MW00563611

True Tales
of
TENNESSEE

True Tales
of
TENNESSEE

EARTHQUAKE TO RAILROAD

BILL CAREY

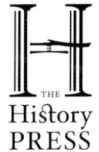

THE
History
PRESS

Published by The History Press
Charleston, SC
www.historypress.com

Copyright © 2023 by Bill Carey
All rights reserved

First published 2023

Manufactured in the United States

ISBN 9781467153898

Library of Congress Control Number: 2022949585

Notice: The information in this book is true and complete to the best of our knowledge. It is offered without guarantee on the part of the author or The History Press. The author and The History Press disclaim all liability in connection with the use of this book.

All rights reserved. No part of this book may be reproduced or transmitted in any form whatsoever without prior written permission from the publisher except in the case of brief quotations embodied in critical articles and reviews.

CONTENTS

CONTENTS

INTRODUCTION

*T*here have been many changes during the last forty-four years. It's 2023 as I write this, and I'm old enough to remember what life was like more than half a century ago. Since 1979, we've seen the development of the internet and cellular phones—both of which meant staggering changes in communication, our pace of life, how we get our news and how we navigate. We've seen improvements in transportation, allowing more people to go on weekend getaways and faraway vacations. We've seen improvements in medical care—a cancer diagnosis that was fatal in 1979 may not be fatal today. We've seen changes in music, changes in conversation, changes in movies. We've seen the fall of the Iron Curtain, shifts in what political parties stand for and an increased awareness of the damage that humans are doing to our planet and climate.

However, the changes we have seen in the last half century are nothing in comparison to the changes Tennesseans experienced in the first half of the nineteenth century.

In 1810, to get from one place to another, Tennesseans had to walk, float downstream, paddle upstream, ride a horse or use some sort of horse-drawn conveyance. As a result of this, average people rarely ventured farther than the next county (unless they were moving from one place to another, which for many people was the longest journey of their lives).

In 1810, it took weeks for people to receive news. Print newspapers were delivered by stagecoach, which—as I explain in this book—moved incredibly slowly. In 1812, when war broke out between Great Britain and the United States, it took more than a month for the news to make its way to households throughout Tennessee. Three years later, the Battle of New Orleans occurred six weeks after the peace treaty ended the War of 1812 because it took news so long to be spread.

In 1810, Tennessee had a population of about 250,000. The state reached from the Appalachian Mountains in the East to where the Tennessee River flows north, at the western edge of what was still known as the Mero District. The state had thirty-nine counties.

In 1810, Tennessee residents could not conceive the idea of photography. If you wanted an image created of yourself, you had to draw one or hire a portrait painter.

Fast-forward from 1810 to 1854. In that year, to get from one place to another, many Tennesseans could ride a train or take a steamboat. Starting on January 17, 1854—the date on which (I have concluded) the first locomotive made it all the way from Nashville to Chattanooga—a person could travel from Middle Tennessee to the Atlantic Ocean in about a day and a half.

In 1854, the national news items reported in the newspapers in Nashville, Memphis, Knoxville and Chattanooga would have all been sent by telegraph from New York, Philadelphia and Washington, D.C. It was quite possible for a person to know news from far away that had taken place only hours earlier.

In 1854, Tennessee had a population of more than 1 million. The state reached from the Appalachian Mountains to the Mississippi River. Tennessee had eighty-two counties, and very few people even remembered what the words "Mero District" meant.

In 1854, Tennesseans were used to the idea that they had some say in how the United States was run. After all, two of its residents—Andrew Jackson and James K. Polk—had been president for about half of the previous quarter century.

By 1854, almost all Tennessee residents had read about photography and even seen photographs. Thanks to the fact that there were professional photographers in towns as small as Fayetteville and Athens, it was very possible for even ordinary Tennesseans to have their picture taken.

These remarkable changes are at the heart of this book.

I originally researched most of these topics in my roles as the executive director of Tennessee History for Kids and as a columnist for *Tennessee Magazine*. Tennessee History for Kids is the nonprofit organization that I cofounded in 2004 to help public school teachers teach social studies. *Tennessee Magazine* is the monthly publication of the Tennessee Electric Cooperatives Association.

For the fact that I'm able to make my living doing this, I want to thank Tennessee History for Kids' board members, its sponsors, the General Assembly and Tennessee's public school teachers and students. I also want to thank my family for tolerating my unusual profession.

I hope that you find this book meaningful, and I hope it awakens in you an appreciation of our state and its history.

GROUND RISES AND FALLS

*A*t about 2:00 a.m. on December 16, 1811, the ground began to shake uncontrollably. Large trees swayed and then snapped throughout Missouri, Kentucky, Arkansas, Tennessee, Illinois and other states. Steep bluffs tumbled into the Mississippi River, which overflowed its banks and appeared to flow backward in places. Cracks in the ground appeared, some of them miles long and wide enough to swallow deer and bears. Black rocks as heavy as thirty pounds shot into the air through holes that instantaneously developed in the ground.

Today, we refer to this as the New Madrid earthquake. But it wasn't a single event; it was a series of quakes that started in December 1811 and continued through March 1812. In fact, based on the records of a learned Louisville, Kentucky resident named Jared Brooks, who built a series of pendulums to document the events, there were 1,874 different quakes. The three most severe are believed to have been on December 16, January 23 and February 7, and those three are each estimated to have measured in excess of 7.5 on the Richter scale.

In terms of area affected, the New Madrid earthquakes were the most dramatic in American history. They were felt strongly over fifty thousand square miles—nearly ten times the land affected by the 1906 San Francisco earthquake. People felt the quakes in places such as Detroit, Michigan; Washington, D.C.; and Charleston, South Carolina. "The vibration was so great as to set the housebells and the bell of St. Philip's Church ringing, and the furniture in motion, some of which in several houses, was thrown down," the *Charleston Daily Courier* reported on December 17, 1811.

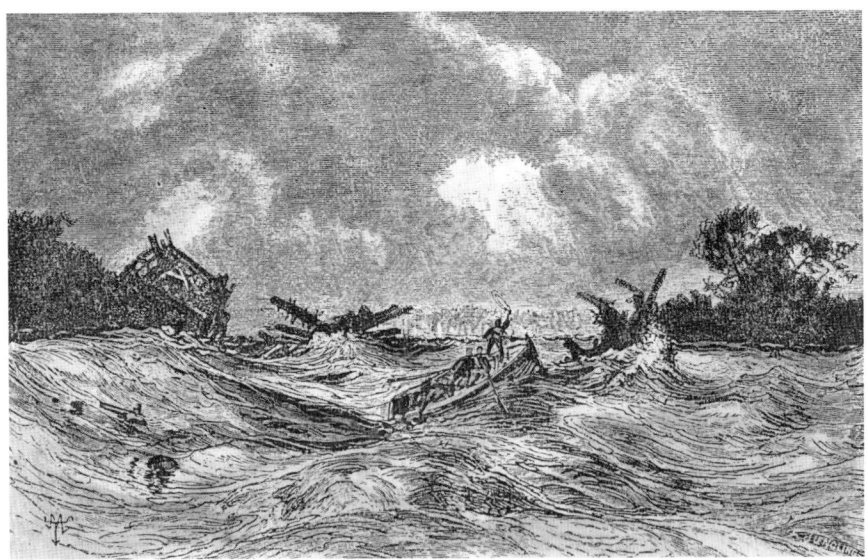

This engraving shows the Mississippi River during the New Madrid earthquakes. *Grainger Historical Archive.*

The New Madrid earthquakes also left permanent marks on the Tennessee landscape. Several islands that had been mapped on the Mississippi River vanished. The subtle fifteen- to thirty-foot rise in the terrain on which the town of Tiptonville sits, known as the Tiptonville Dome, is believed to have been made higher by the quakes. East of Tiptonville, water poured into a swampy area that sank several feet, creating Reelfoot Lake.

We have no idea how many people lost their lives due to the New Madrid earthquakes because the territory was so sparsely populated and because communication was not good at the time. We know there were some deaths. Timothy Flint, a Presbyterian minister living in New Madrid, Missouri, recalled that "one woman, frightened by the shock, ran until her strength ran out and expired by fear and exhaustion." People who were on or near the Mississippi River saw flatboats and canoes drift by with no one in them and thus made the assumption that everyone on board had been swept away and drowned.

But anecdotes about loss of life were rare and could not be confirmed at the time. All of West Tennessee was Chickasaw land then; we have no idea how many members of the Chickasaw Nation perished in the earthquakes.

Because the New Madrid earthquakes occurred so long ago, we also have no photographs to document what took place. We have a few first-person accounts of what people felt, heard, saw, smelled and feared.

There aren't many of these accounts, and for the most part it isn't clear which of the quakes or tremors people are talking about when they recollected the events years later. But the accounts tell a vivid story of what the catastrophe was like.

Eliza Bryan, a resident of New Madrid, said that early in the morning of December 16, 1811, "we were visited by a violent shock of an earthquake, accompanied by a very awful noise, resembling loud but distant thunder, but more hoarse and vibrating which was followed in a few minutes by the complete saturation of the atmosphere with sulphurous vapor....The screams of the affrighted inhabitants running to and fro, not knowing where to go or what to do—the cries of the fowl and the beasts of every species, the cracking of trees falling and the roaring of the Mississippi River...formed a scene truly terrible."

The "sulphurous vapor" Bryan mentioned was a chemical released by the earth that engulfed the entire region with a fog-like covering for months. Another resident of New Madrid said after the first quake struck, "We sought a high open spot of ground, and remained there until morning, which it seemed to us would never come. When morning dawned, no sun shone on

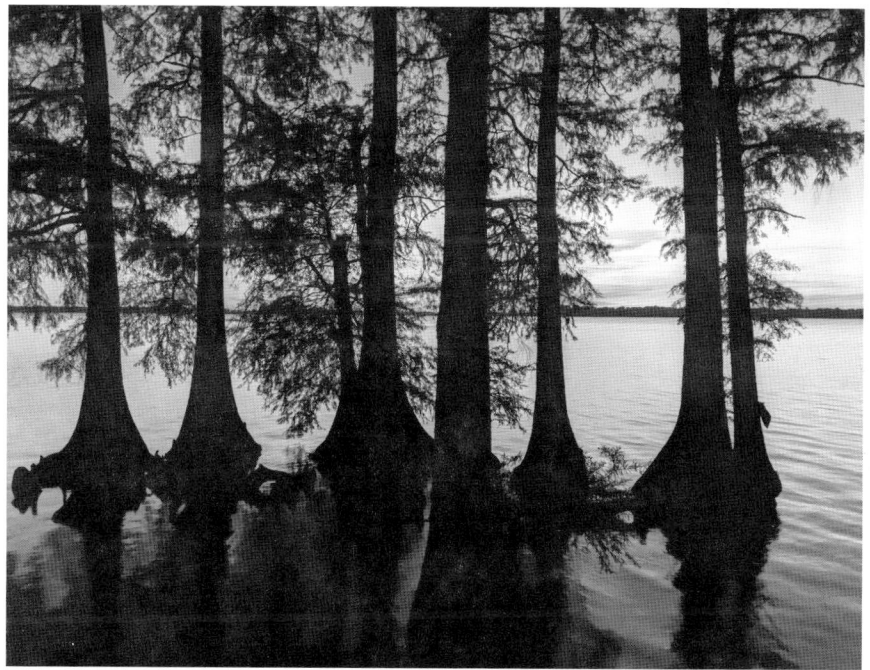

Reelfoot Lake. *Author's collection.*

us to gladden our hearts. A dense vapor arose from the seams of the earth and hid it from view."

Descriptions of the noises made by the earth itself differed. Father Joseph, a priest in New Madrid, said the ground "was sometimes muffled and groaning; sometimes it cracked and crashed, not like thunder, but as though a great sheet of ice had broken."

The Mississippi River was an especially dangerous place during the earthquakes and in places had a "turbid and boiling appearance," one traveler said. Firmin La Roche was the commander of three flatboats taking goods from St. Louis to New Orleans. When the quakes began, he reported that "the trees on the shore were falling down and great masses of earth tumbled into the river…in a moment so great a wave came up the river that I never seen one like it at sea. It carried us back north, upstream, for more than a mile, and the water spread out upon the banks, covering maybe three or four miles inland. It was the current going backward."

Many things are submerged in the Mississippi, and some of them shot out of the river as if they'd been fired out of a cannon. Another riverman said that "near our boat, a spout of confined air, breaking its way through the waters, burst forth, and with a loud report discharged mud, sticks, etc. above the surface.…Large trees, which had lain for ages at the very bottom of the river, were shot up in thousands of instances, some with their roots uppermost, and with their tops planted."

Animals have a strange way of knowing about natural disasters before people do, and this one was no different. Artist John James Audubon was riding somewhere in Kentucky when his horse stopped and began acting as if something was wrong, placing "one foot after another on the ground, with as much precaution as if walking on a smooth sheet of ice." A few moments later, "all the shrubs and trees began to move from their very roots. The ground rose and fell in successive furrows, like the ruffled waters of a lake."

As I read the various accounts and contemplated the primitive nature of American civilization at the time, I could not help but wonder about the emotional state of people who endured the earthquakes and tremors. "In faraway Richmond, Virginia, people 'staggered as they stood,'" James Penick said in the 1981 book *The New Madrid Earthquakes*. "In Savannah, Georgia, they were 'made to totter, as if on shipboard'; near Hodgenville, Kentucky, they felt 'light-headed' and reeled about 'like a drunken man.'"

Most people in New Madrid fled to higher ground about forty miles north. John Shaw, a hunter from Wisconsin, found the place where many of the residents of New Madrid had fled. Not surprisingly, they prayed when they got there. "Here the fugitives formed an encampment. It was proposed that all should kneel, and engage in supplicating God's mercy, and all simultaneously, Catholics and Protestants, knelt and offered solemn prayer to their Creator."

Only weeks before the first big quake, people had begun seeing the Great Comet of 1811 move across the sky. John Bradbury, an English naturalist, said he heard one of the men on his flatboat telling everyone the quake was attributed to the comet, "which he described as having two horns, over one of which the earth had rolled, and was now lodged betwixt them; that the shocks were occasioned by the attempts made by the earth to surmount the other horn."

However, one tidbit from Myron Fuller's 1912 government report *The New Madrid Earthquake* makes me think people were thinking clearer than Bradbury may have realized. You see, the long cracks in the ground that were caused by the quakes had a tendency to stretch in the same direction. It crossed the minds of many people that big trees, toppled at right angles to these cracks, might be the safest thing to cling to during a tremor. Upon these very tree trunks "they climbed for safety at times of severe shocks when new fissures were to be expected."

I am strangely comforted by the idea of our ancestors holding on for dear life to these logs, knowing they were doing so for very logical reasons.

UP PAST THE SHOALS

*W*hen settlers crossed the Appalachian Mountains, they left behind the Atlantic Ocean watershed for a land where every river flowed west and south to the Gulf of Mexico. This geographic fact stunted the economy of early Tennessee, but it wouldn't stunt it for long.

You see, in 1807 Robert Fulton drove his new steamboat (then known as the *North River Steamboat*) upstream on New York's Hudson River. Within a few years of that event, steamboats made their way along the Mississippi, Cumberland and Tennessee Rivers. But it took a lot longer for some parts of Tennessee to see the steamboat than it did others.

This isn't one story, but three.

MEMPHIS

The first steamboat to descend the Mississippi River almost certainly stopped at the site of present-day Memphis. In 1810, Robert Fulton and Robert Livingston financed the construction of a steamboat in Pittsburgh, Pennsylvania, called the *New Orleans*. It set off down the Ohio River on October 11, 1811, and probably stopped in late December at the Chickasaw Bluffs of the Mississippi River—site of a trading post at that time—on its maiden voyage to New Orleans.

When I first heard about this journey, I visualized a small boat with barely enough room for a few people—sort of like the one Humphrey Bogart steers

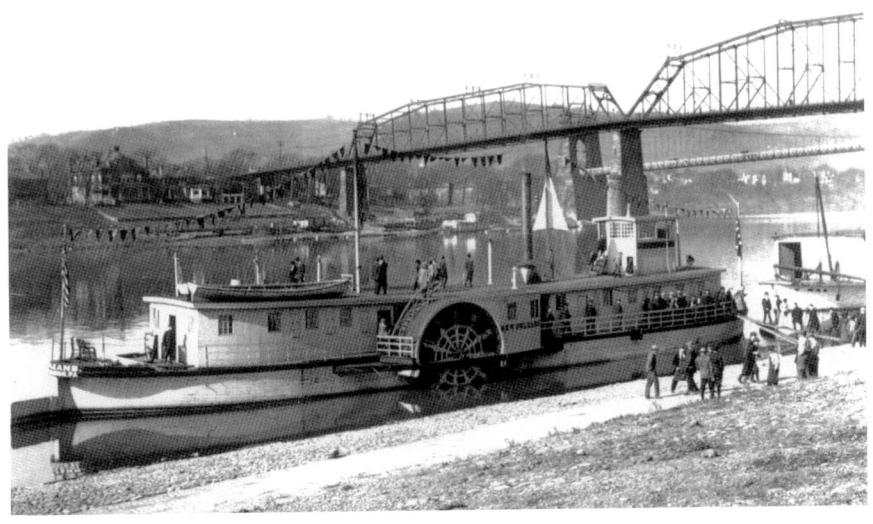

The replica of the *New Orleans* that floated down the Ohio and Mississippi Rivers on the 100th anniversary of its maiden journey. *John Bowman.*

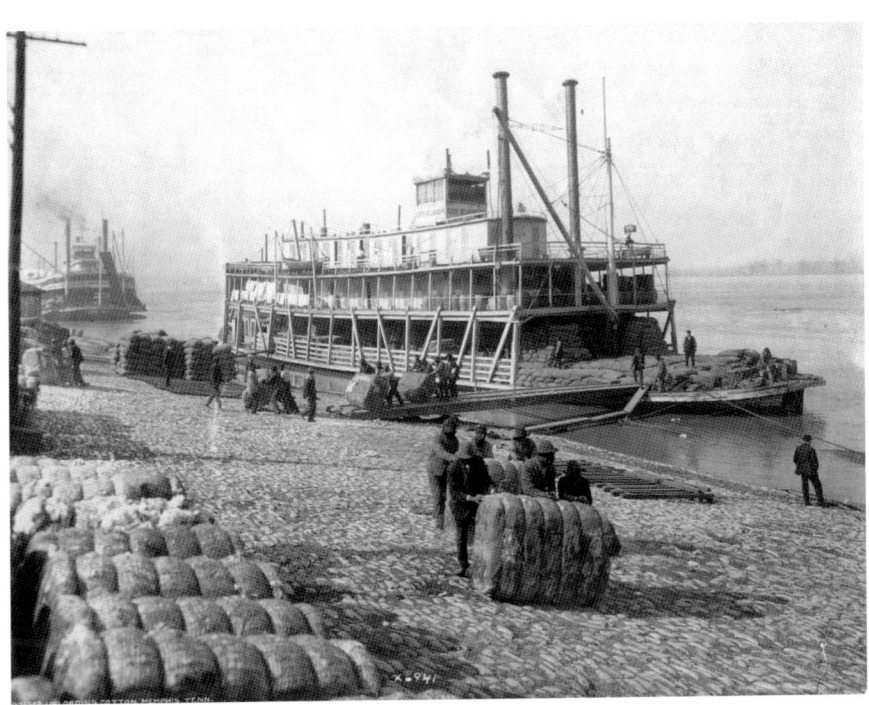

A steamboat in Memphis. *Tennessee State Library and Archives.*

in *The African Queen*. In fact, the *New Orleans* was about 150 feet long and had separate enclosed living spaces for men and women. The boat was propelled by two steam-driven paddlewheels on both sides of the boat.

The *New Orleans* had eight people on board during this maiden voyage: Captain Nicholas Roosevelt; his wife, Lydia; a pilot named Andrew Jack; five deckhands and servants; and a massive Newfoundland named Tiger. In the weeks preceding their stop at the Chickasaw Bluffs, the boat, crew and passengers encountered the treacherous Falls of the Ohio River, hostile Native Americans, the Great Comet of 1811 and (worst of all) the New Madrid earthquakes.

Assuming the *New Orleans* stopped at the Chickasaw Bluffs, the boat didn't stay long because the crew was trying to get to Natchez as fast as it could.

The Chickasaw Indians would relinquish their claims on West Tennessee in 1818, and it was about that time that three men (one of whom was Andrew Jackson) organized the town of Memphis. Memphis would rapidly become a stop for steamboats on the Mississippi River. As farmers in West Tennessee, Northern Mississippi and Arkansas adopted cotton as their main crop, Memphis emerged as the cotton trading capital of the inland United States, and it did so thanks to steamboats.

NASHVILLE

There used to be a long stretch of shallow water on the Cumberland River about twenty-five miles downstream from Nashville called the Harpeth Shoals. Because of this, it wasn't easy to get a steamboat to Nashville.

Every Tennessee history book and article I've ever seen claims the *General Jackson* was the first steamboat to make it up the Cumberland River to Nashville. However, I now believe that every history book and article was wrong.

A prominent Nashville merchant named Christopher Stump published a large advertisement in the June 23, 1818 issue of the Nashville *Clarion and Tennessee Gazette* newspaper. In the ad, Stump claimed he had groceries, fabric and hardware to sell which he had "just received from the steamboat *Constitution.*"

There was, in fact, a steamboat called the *Constitution* built in Pittsburgh and launched in 1816. It was originally called the *Oliver Evans* but was renamed after a deadly explosion in 1817.

I believe the reason the *General Jackson* was more talked about in Nashville is that it was locally owned (by former governor William Carroll, among

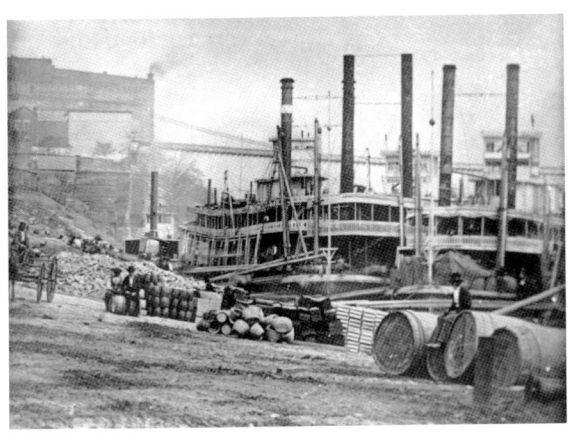

A steamboat in Nashville.
Tennessee State Library and Archives.

others). That would account for why its arrival in March 1819 was more of a civic event than the *Constitution*'s arrival the year before.

Regardless of whether the *Constitution* or *General Jackson* was first, Nashville's economy quickly adapted to the steamboat. The Harpeth Shoals remained a problem; from July to October, the Cumberland was so shallow on the shoals that boats would often get stuck there. Crafts often unloaded their goods below the shoals and delivered them by wagon to Nashville.

The Harpeth Shoals would remain an impediment on the Cumberland River until a dam created by the U.S. Army Corps of Engineers flooded it permanently in 1904.

CHATTANOOGA AND KNOXVILLE

Steamboats did not reach Chattanooga and Knoxville until seventeen years after they reached Memphis and a decade after they reached Nashville. This is because of the many navigational obstacles on the Tennessee River, such as the Muscle Shoals in northwest Alabama and the series of unpredictable features in the river in southeast Tennessee with names such as the Suck and the Boiling Pot.

Steamboats were expensive, and none of their financiers was eager to risk their boats on the Muscle Shoals and the Suck. Therefore, authorities in Knoxville offered to pay $640 to the first steamboat that made it to that city.

A steamboat called the *Atlas* wasn't the first to try, but it was the first to succeed. Around January 20, 1828, the *Atlas* made it through the Muscle Shoals with less trouble than had been expected. "We understand that is intended to take out her engine and work the empty boat over the rapids," the *Knoxville Enquirer* first said. However, the boat made it through the Muscle Shoals without having to take this step. A few weeks later, the *Atlas* made it through the Boiling Pot and the Suck to the present-day site of Chattanooga (a Cherokee trading post called Ross's Landing at the time).

A lot of people turned out in Knoxville to greet the steamboat when it arrived on March 4. By that late date, many of Knoxville's business leaders realized steamboats would have a limited effect on their city's commerce. After all, 1828 was the year the Baltimore and Ohio broke ground on the railroad that would eventually connect the Atlantic Ocean to the Ohio River. The B&O turned the attention of every American city on the Mississippi River system—from Cincinnati to Louisville to Knoxville—to the idea of the railroad.

Because river access was impeded by the Muscle Shoals and the Suck, Knoxville would never really become a big steamboat town. It would eventually be a big railroad town, but that's another story!

ATTACK AT THE BEND

Some of the more important events in Tennessee history didn't occur in Tennessee.

On March 27, 1814, an army led by Andrew Jackson and consisting of, among others, nearly two thousand volunteer soldiers from Tennessee attacked a Creek stronghold in what is now Tallapoosa County, Alabama. The victory by Jackson's army at Horseshoe Bend meant the end of the Creek (Muskogee) Nation's power east of the Mississippi River and resulted in the annexation of 23 million acres of land for the United States. It also resulted in immediate fame for Jackson and was his first major step toward the presidency.

So why did the Battle of Horseshoe Bend take place? It's a long story. Keep in mind that it took place during the War of 1812—in which the British encouraged Native Americans to fight against the United States. It happened a few years after the Shawnee chief Tecumseh came south and encouraged other Native American nations to fight against settlers. And it occurred when the American government was trying to "civilize" Native Americans and blaze a new road through Creek territory—steps to which many Creeks objected.

Not all of the Creeks took up arms against the U.S. Army in 1813 and 1814. Those who did are generally referred to as Red Sticks, and starting in February 1813, there were several military engagements between Red Sticks and the U.S. Army.

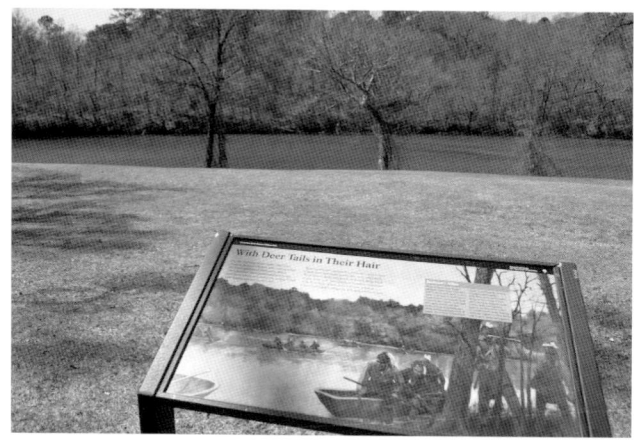

Horseshoe Bend
National Military
Park in Alabama.
Author's collection.

Prior to Horseshoe Bend, the best known of these took place at Fort Mims, near what is now Mobile, Alabama, in August 1813. At Fort Mims, an army of about 1,000 Red Sticks killed an estimated 250 settlers—among them women and children. "Remember Fort Mims" thus became the rallying cry for Americans who came to fight the Creeks.

By March 1814, the Red Sticks, led by a warrior named Menawa, had set up a stronghold near a Creek town called Tohopeka. Surrounded on the west, south and east by the Tallapoosa River and protected on the north by a long log barricade, Menawa's thousand warriors believed their defenses to be more than adequate. But only about one-third of them possessed muskets; the rest were armed with bows, arrows, tomahawks and warclubs.

Jackson's army of 3,300 men consisted of the Thirty-Ninth U.S. Infantry Regiment, several groups of militia from Tennessee, 500 Cherokee warriors and about 100 Creek warriors opposed to the Red Sticks. Jackson's plan was to blast the log barricade using the two small cannons and then attack the barricade with the infantry. If and when the Creeks tried to retreat across the river, they would be met by sharpshooters from Tennessee, commanded by General John Coffee, and by the Cherokee warriors—who were all stationed across the Tallapoosa River.

Wary of deserters and undisciplined soldiers, Jackson told his men he would not tolerate disobedience. "Any officer or soldier who flies before the enemy without being compelled to do so by superior force and actual necessity shall suffer death," he told his men in advance of the battle.

Things didn't, however, go according to plans. At 10:30 a.m., Jackson's cannons opened fire. For nearly two hours, shells landed on or near the barricade but did not appear to blast holes in it, as Jackson had hoped. But as soon as they heard the cannon fire, the Cherokee and Creek warriors allied to the Americans decided to cross the river and attack on their own, which they did with considerable success. General Jackson only became aware of this when he saw smoke rising from the burning village. Jackson then ordered his infantry to attack the barricade on foot.

Fighting was fierce, most of it hand to hand. "Arrows, spears and balls were flying," one participant later wrote, "swords and tomahawks were gleaming in the sun." One of the first Americans killed in this charge was Major Lemuel Montgomery. His tombstone is now the only marked grave on the battlefield.

Creek warriors at the barricade were soon overwhelmed, and those who weren't killed immediately retreated—some to protect their village from the Cherokee attack that had come from the rear and some to get away from the infantry assault in the front. The battle soon deteriorated into a slaughter. Many Creek warriors found it impossible to defend their village and, unwilling to surrender, tried to cross the Tallapoosa River. Practically all of them who tried to cross the river were shot by Coffee's sharpshooters from Tennessee. So many died crossing the river, in fact, that the river is said to have been red with blood.

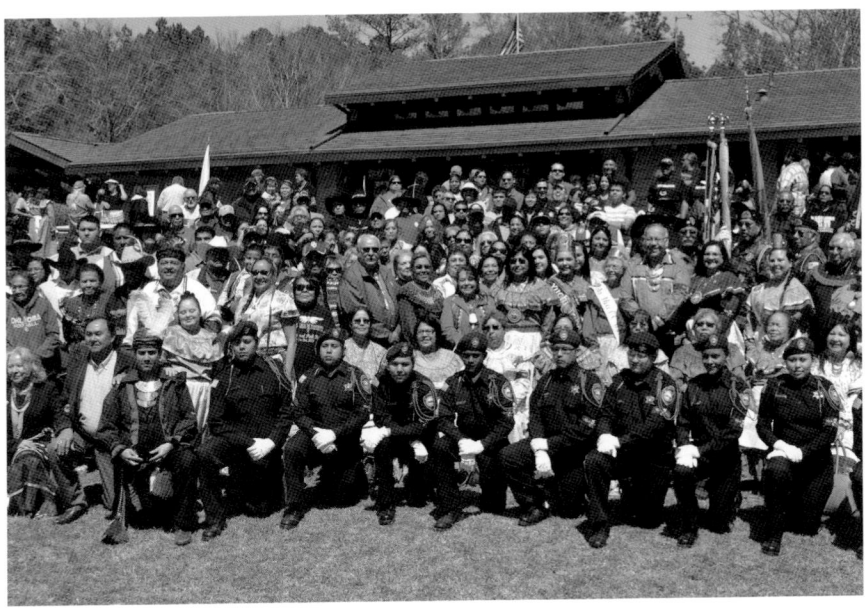

A large group of dignitaries from the Muskogee Indian Nation in Oklahoma visited Horseshoe Bend on the 200th anniversary of the battle in 2014. *Author's collection.*

Today, we estimate that eight hundred Creeks died—the largest death toll for Native Americans in a single battle in American history. On the U.S. side, twenty-six soldiers were killed, while eighteen Cherokees and five Creeks who fought with them also died.

A few months later, in August 1814, the Creeks signed the Treaty of Fort Jackson, ceding much of what is now central and southern Alabama and southern Georgia to the United States.

Now for a few points of interest about this battle:

Practically none of the Creek warriors surrendered; they either managed to escape or chose to fight to the death. However, many Creek women and children in the village of Tohopeka did surrender.

The U.S. Army apparently left the dead Creek warriors, unburied, on the battlefield and buried their own dead (other than Major Montgomery) in the Tallapoosa River.

Among the troops who attacked the Creek barricade that day was a young officer named Sam Houston. He fought on in spite of the fact that he was hit by an arrow in his thigh and then was hit twice by musket balls. That night, Houston assumed he was done for. "I received less attention than the others [meaning the other wounded soldiers], for everyone looked on me as a dying man, and what could be done for any, they felt should be done for those who were likely to live," he late wrote in his autobiography. "It was the darkest night of my life." Houston was later elected governor of Tennessee and Texas.

Coffee County is named for General John Coffee.

Montgomery County, Alabama, is named for Lemuel Montgomery.

Finally, during the Indian Removal of 1830s, many Cherokees bitterly recalled how their nation fought *with* Andrew Jackson at the Battle of Horseshoe Bend. In fact, over the years there emerged a story that the Cherokee warrior Junaluska actually saved Jackson's life during the battle.

There is no question that the Cherokees played an important part in the battle, but there is no evidence that Junaluska saved Jackson's life at Horseshoe Bend. During the battle, Jackson was not believed to be in any personal danger and remained in a safe place directing his army.

VICTORY OF THE DIRTY SHIRTS

A few years ago, I found a brochure for a New Orleans museum that helped me understand the importance of the Battle of New Orleans.

"In the waning days of the War of 1812," began the brochure for the Historic New Orleans Collection, "Andrew Jackson shocked the world by leading a ragtag force of local and state militia, regular U.S. troops, free men of color, Choctaw Indians and Baratarian pirates to a crushing victory of an invading army of proud, tested, elite British soldiers determined to seize New Orleans."

In the fall of 1814, fifteen thousand British troops and fifty ships invaded Louisiana. These were experienced soldiers who had previously fought Napoleon. They were so confident that their commander, Admiral Alexander Cochrane, said he intended to give the Americans "a complete drubbing."

Since practically all goods produced west of the Appalachian Mountains had to pass through New Orleans to get to open seas, this was a major threat to the United States. In the months leading up to this, General Andrew Jackson's army of state militias and regular U.S. troops had fought battles against Creek Indians in present-day Alabama and against the Spanish in present-day Florida. With the British coming, the U.S. government ordered Jackson's army to defend New Orleans.

Jackson's army marched down the Natchez Trace and then through New Orleans. After a brief, minor engagement with the British on December 23,

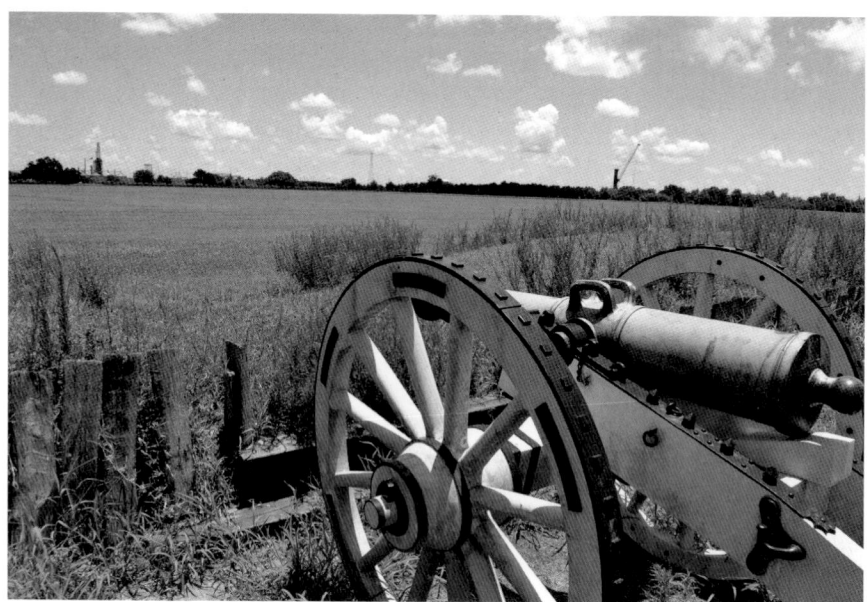

Chalmette National Historical Park near New Orleans. *Author's collection.*

Jackson's men set up at a sugar plantation called Chalmette, about five miles south of the city. Jackson chose a narrow stretch of land, with the Mississippi River on one side and a swamp on the other. He ordered his men to dig a ditch, build a rampart behind it and set up eight artillery batteries for defense. They waited for the main British attack, which came on January 8, 1815.

On paper, this looked like a mismatch favoring the British. Jackson's army was outnumbered three to one. About 1,300 of his men were militia from Tennessee, many of whom had fought at Horseshoe Bend. He had a few hundred soldiers from the U.S. Army. He had Louisiana militiamen, many of whom spoke French and Spanish but not English. He had 62 Choctaw Indians. He had a group of privateers from Louisiana known as Baratarians.

Jackson also had nearly five hundred free Black men fighting for him at New Orleans. In fact, this was the largest use of free Black men in an American battle until the Civil War.

The British had more soldiers, more experienced soldiers and better trained soldiers than Jackson had. When the British soldiers charged into the American lines on January 8, 1815, they could have rightfully thought they would defeat the Americans with ease. But the British commanders, such as Admiral Cochrane and General Edward Pakenham, made terrible mistakes that day.

For instance, at the beginning of the day, a British force crossed the Mississippi River intending to march upstream and fire guns across the river at the American lines. But they didn't realize how strong the river current was. When they set off to cross the river, they drifted downstream. The crossing took hours longer than it was supposed to; by the time they got across the river from Chalmette, the battle was over.

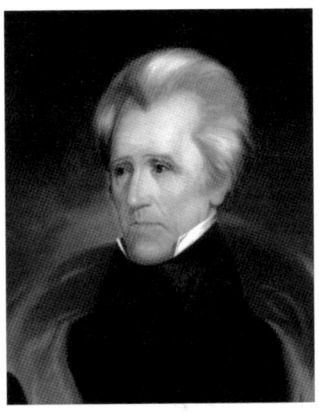

Andrew Jackson. *Ralph E. W. Earl, artist.*

Also, when the main battle began, the British assumed that the weak point of the American line were the "dirty shirts"—the men from Tennessee and Kentucky who didn't have real uniforms. However, many of these "dirty shirts" had fought together for years and were fine soldiers. As the British soldiers marched toward them, they were mowed down by the "dirty shirts," who were led by Tennessee generals Coffee and Carroll (for whom Coffee and Carroll Counties are named).

Finally, the ladders and bases the British soldiers had intended to use to climb over the American ramparts simply never got to the front lines. Hundreds of British soldiers died standing in formation, waiting for ladders that never came.

In one of the most lopsided battles to ever take place in world history, Andrew Jackson's army crushed the British in the Battle of New Orleans. More than two thousand British soldiers were killed, wounded, captured or missing. General Pakenham was also killed, shot several times on the battlefield. In a letter to James Monroe several years later, Jackson described what he saw: "I heard a single rifle shot from a group of country carts we had been using, and a moment thereafter I saw Pakenham reel and pitch out of his saddle....I have always believed he fell from the bullet of a free man of color, who was a famous rifle shot and came from the Attakapas region of Louisiana." Thus a major general in the British army and the brother-in-law of the Duke of Wellington met his fate—shot near New Orleans by a free Black man from Louisiana under the command of Tennessean who was left destitute when he lost his mother and brothers in the Revolutionary War.

The Americans lost about twenty men in the battle.

So, why do many textbooks downplay the Battle of New Orleans? The peace treaty ending the War of 1812 had already been signed in Belgium back on December 14, 1814—about two weeks before the Battle of New Orleans took place. (In those days, it took a long time for news to be delivered.)

In spite of this, some historians believe the Battle of New Orleans did change American history. After all, the lopsided nature of the battle may have ensured that the British would never fight a war against the United States again. Also, the battle certainly made General Andrew Jackson a national hero. His leadership in battle had a lot to do with why he was elected president in 1828.

For many years, January 8 was celebrated as a national holiday in the United States. They still acknowledge the day in Louisiana.

Any account of the Battle of New Orleans has to mention that the site of the battle was extensively flooded by Hurricane Katrina in 2005. Chalmette Medical Center closed after Katrina—never to reopen—and the neighborhoods in the area have still not returned to its pre-Katrina levels. However, the Chalmette National Battlefield is a wonderful place to visit, and the people at Rocky and Carlos Restaurant down the street were as hospitable as they could be. They also gave me about three times as much to eat for lunch as any sane person would want to eat. But what happens in New Orleans stays in New Orleans.

LIFE SHROUDED IN MYSTERY

Sequoyah is one of the most important Tennesseans and one of the most important members of the Cherokee Nation to have ever lived. He created a syllabary, one symbol at a time, which allowed a person to write down any Cherokee word. This enabled the Cherokee people to become the first American Indians to have a written language.

It was a remarkable achievement. "Sequoyah is the only person in recorded history who created a writing system without first knowing a written language himself," said Dr. Duane King, director of the Helmerich Center for American Research at the Gilcrease Museum in Tulsa, Oklahoma.

So, why does writing about Sequoyah scare me? Because much of what is written about the man contradicts itself. No matter what history book or children's book you read, no matter what video you watch, no matter which website you click on, you will find different accounts of Sequoyah's life. This is the great irony of Sequoyah. The man who invented a written language never wrote his own story. Stories about his life are all derived from a combination of oral tradition and conjecture.

For instance, we are not certain when Sequoyah was born. Various accounts of his life say he was born anywhere from 1760 until 1778. We do know about *where* he was born—the location is in present-day Monroe County, where you will find the Sequoyah Birthplace Museum.

We are not certain who his parents were. Most sources indicate that Sequoyah's mother was a full-blooded Cherokee named Wut-teh and his father was a fur trader from Maryland named Nathanial Gist (a name that is often spelled "Guess"). But there are other accounts.

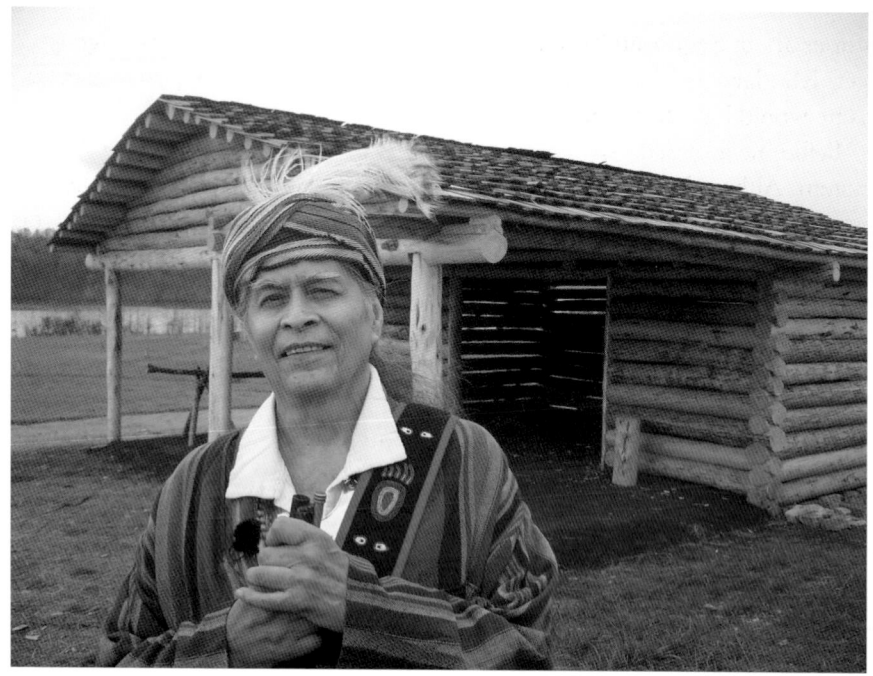

A Sequoyah reenactor. *Sequoyah Birthplace Museum.*

The man himself went by two names. His Cherokee name was Sequoyah. His English name was George Gist (or Guess). This practice of having two names was very common at the time in the Cherokee world in which Sequoyah lived.

Sequoyah had a limp, but we don't know why. Since the name Sequoyah means "pig's foot," many believe he was born with a disability. However, some accounts claim he was injured in a hunting accident or even in military service. "I think I have read twenty-five different accounts of why he limped," said Charlie Rhodarmer, director of the Sequoyah Birthplace Museum in Vonore.

Like many other Cherokees, Sequoyah fought on the American side during the Creek War. His biographers have always assumed, therefore, that he was present at the Battle of Horseshoe Bend on March 27, 1814. However, "just what part Sequoyah played in the fighting is not on record," claimed Stan Hoig, in the book *Sequoyah: The Cherokee Genius*.

Sequoyah was a silversmith and a blacksmith. This means that by standards of the time, he was well off and could buy household necessities as he needed them. "I laugh at the idea which you see in videos and read in stories about Sequoyah having to use knife and bark to create his language," said Rhodarmer. "He would have been able to buy as much pen and paper as he would have liked, and I'm sure he did."

Before he invented his syllabary, Sequoyah may have invented a numbering system. Although we do not know this, it seems logical that the numbering system came out of his need to run his blacksmith business. "I think he invented the numbering system as a way of keeping track of who owed him money, and how much they owed him," said Rhodarmer. "After all, he made his living doing things like making nails, jewelry and tools. He did so at a time when many of his customers couldn't pay when they picked things up. So he had to keep up with all this."

We don't know exactly what led Sequoyah to invent his syllabary. Hoig's book cites several separate explanations, all of which came from secondhand sources produced prior to the 1840s. According to some stories, Sequoyah said he originally got the idea watching American soldiers during the Creek War. However, a story in the *Cherokee Phoenix*, published in 1828, said the idea came to Sequoyah when he overheard a conversation between young men who were talking about the ability of white men to put their language on paper.

"Mr. Guess, after silently listening to their conversation for a while, raised himself, and putting on an air of importance, said, 'You are all fools; why, the thing is very easy; I can do it myself,' and, picking up a flat stone, he commenced scratching on it with a pin; and after a few minutes read to them a sentence, which he had written by making a mark for each word. This produced a laugh, and the conversation on that subject ended. But the inventive powers of Guess's mind were now roused to action; and nothing short of being able to write the Cherokee language would satisfy him. He went home, purchased materials, and sat down to paint the Cherokee language on paper."

We don't know when Sequoyah moved from Tennessee to present-day Alabama. Because of this, no one really knows whether he was already working on the written language when he moved to Alabama or whether the idea came to him after he moved there.

Sequoyah had his share of detractors. All the accounts of Sequoyah's life seem to maintain that many other members of the Cherokee Nation, including his wife, thought he was crazy. At some point, long after Sequoyah started working on his project, she reportedly destroyed all of his work. Sequoyah was frustrated, but he started all over again. "If our people think I am making a fool of myself, you may tell them that what I am doing will not

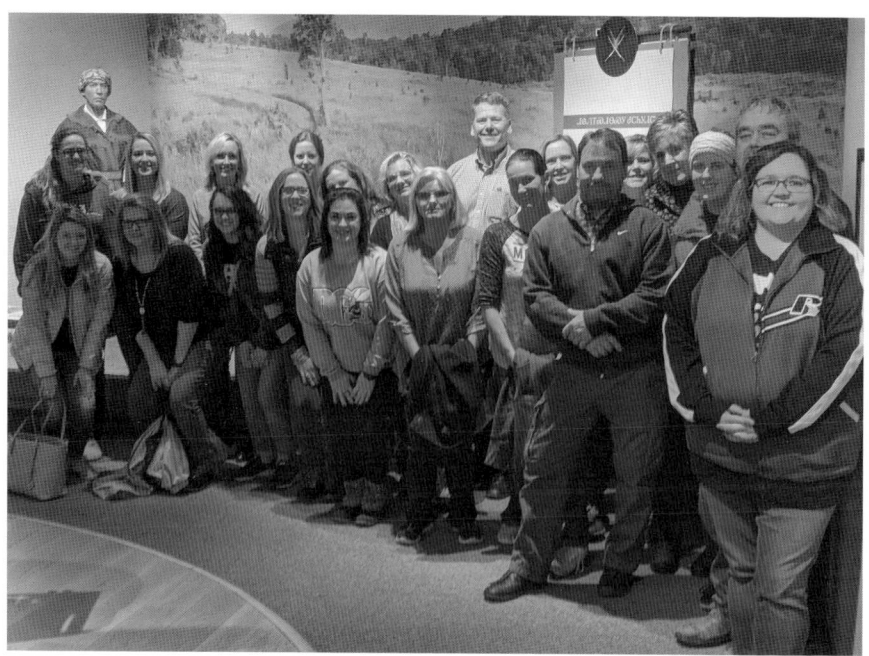

A teacher training event at the Sequoyah Birthplace Museum in Monroe County. *Author's collection.*

make fools of them," Sequoyah said, according to a book called *Old Frontiers* by John P. Brown.

Sequoyah's demonstration of his written language to the Cherokee people was dramatic. Most accounts claim that Sequoyah, under suspicion of witchcraft, demonstrated his written language to tribal elders with the help of his daughter Ayoka. Here's an account of this demonstration from the official website of the Cherokee Nation (www.cherokee.org):

> *Although the system was foolproof and easy to learn, Sequoyah and Ayoka were charged with witchcraft, and were brought before George Lowery, their town chief, for trial. Due to a Cherokee law enacted in 1811, it was mandated to have a civil trial before an execution was allowed to take place. Lowery brought in a group of warriors to judge what was termed a "sorcery trial." For evidence of the literacy claims, the warriors separated Sequoyah and his daughter to have them send messages between each other until they were finally convinced that the symbols on paper really represented talking.*

We do not know when Sequoyah died or where he is buried. We think he died in Mexico, where he was trying to locate Cherokee people who had moved there from the United States.

Finally, I want to point out that none of this uncertainty about Sequoyah's life detracts from the man's significance. In 1825, only four years after he had begun showing it to others, the Cherokee Nation adopted Sequoyah's writing system. With the help of missionaries, they began printing a newspaper in Cherokee called the *Cherokee Phoenix*. Soon the literacy rate of Cherokees was higher than the literacy rate of the settlers in that part of the South. Sequoyah, whom everyone had thought was crazy, was praised not only by his own people but also by the U.S. government and newspapers around the world.

Sadly, Sequoyah's writing system was not enough to keep the Cherokees from being forced to leave their homeland in what is now known at the Trail of Tears. By that time, Sequoyah had moved west, to what is now Oklahoma.

WEALTHY, RESPECTABLE AND POPULOUS

*T*owns didn't just "happen." They were founded by investors who pooled their money, sent surveyors to find the most strategic locations, bought and subdivided hundreds of acres and laid out town squares, roads and parcels. These investors also bought advertisements that made their communities sound like the best places to live.

After the War of 1812, the U.S. government bought land west of the Tennessee River and east of the Mississippi River from the Chickasaw Nation. Andrew Jackson represented the U.S. government in this 1818 transaction, which newspapers of the early nineteenth century referred to as the Chickasaw Purchase. After it occurred, the Chickasaw Indians were forced to move to present-day Mississippi.

Settlers from the east moved quickly into West Tennessee, creating one of America's first land rushes. They organized towns with speed—a process documented in newspapers of the time. The first-ever mentions of these towns in newspapers were advertisements explaining where the town would be created, what types of natural resources it boasted and other enticements.

One of the first ads appeared in newspapers as far away as Pennsylvania. "[The] town of Memphis has been laid off by the proprietors on the Chickasaw Bluff, on the east bank of the Mississippi, 224 miles below the mouth of the Ohio," reported the July 1820 *Pittsburgh Weekly Gazette*. "The site of this town is believed to be the handsomest on the Mississippi below St. Louis."

TOWN OF MEMPHIS,

HAS been laid off by the proprietors on the Chickasaw Bluff, on the east bank of the Mississippi, 224 miles below the mouth of the Ohio. The position is noticed in the Pittsburgh Navigator, p. 165. The site of this town is believed to be the handsomest on the Mississippi below St. Louis.

It is the intention of the propietors not to offer the Lots at public sale, but to induce, and make it the interest of the prudent and discreet adventurers of all classes, to settle and improve the place. The plan for its settlement was not decided on until the 26th inst. when it was determined by the proprietors to dispose of no lots except to actual settlers for a reasonable consideration, payable at the end of five years, on bond, and security if required, to be given at the end of that time. The situation is handsome, well watered, and healty. It is situated in lat. 35°6 N. long. 13'W. from Washington, according to Melish's map. Its position and advantages invite the community particularly, to examine it and judge for themselves.

The proprietors have agents resident at that place, viz : major Marcus B. Winchester, Dr. W. Butler and William Lawrence, any two of whom are authorised to transact business ; to whom application can be made, and by whom the terms of settlement and sale, will be more particularly made known.

John Overton,

acting for himself and other members of the company.
Nashville, T. May 13.

Pittsburgh Weekly Gazette, July 24, 1820.

The ad went on to describe the location of Memphis as 35 degrees, 6 minutes north latitude, 13 degrees west longitude "from Washington"—a reminder that, in 1820, the United States refused to go along with a longitudinal system centered on a country against which it had fought two wars.

During the next few years, the *Jackson Gazette* contained ads for many other new towns in West Tennessee. "On Monday the 20th of September next, the Commissioners of the town of Lexington will proceed to sell the balance of the LOTS remaining unsold in said town," the paper reported in August 1824.

"The measure of [Brownsville's] population is filling up with a rapidity unparalleled," claimed an ad in January 1825, "and we presume the day is not far distant, when, on account of its wealth and the character of its inhabitants, it will be considered inferior to none."

"Among the many towns about to be reared in the Western District, none presents greater claims to public consideration than the town of Covington," claimed an ad in February 1825. "Few towns in the state possess equal advantages in a commercial point of view."

"Taking everything into view, we feel ourselves authorized in saying the town of Dresden presents to the purchaser many advantages, and has a fair prospect of becoming wealthy, respectable and populous," noted an ad in February 1825.

"This town [Gibson-Port] is situated on a beautiful eminence, or bluff, on the South side of the Little North Fork of Forked-Deer River, in the centre of a county in point of soil not surpassed by any in the Western District," the *Gazette* published in June 1825. (Gibson-Port later changed its name to Trenton.)

"We believe few town sites in the Western country will present to the consideration of the people superior claims [than that of Dyersburg]," said an ad in July 1825.

"This town [Somerville] is beautifully situated on Loos Hatchie River, near never-failing water, and also near the centre of a county affording large bodies of excellent land," stated another ad in the *Gazette* in July 1825.

All of these towns remain today, although it's safe to say that most of them didn't meet the grandiose dreams of their founders. Following are some examples of places that were announced with great fanfare but simply ceased to exist after the emergence of railroads.

PURDY. The original county seat of McNairy County, Purdy was announced in February 1825. "There will be sold on the 30th of March next, and the succeeding days, in the town of Purdy, and county of McNairy, the lots of said town," the *Nashville Whig* said. "As to beauty of situation it is equaled by few and surpassed by none, and is without a doubt the healthiest

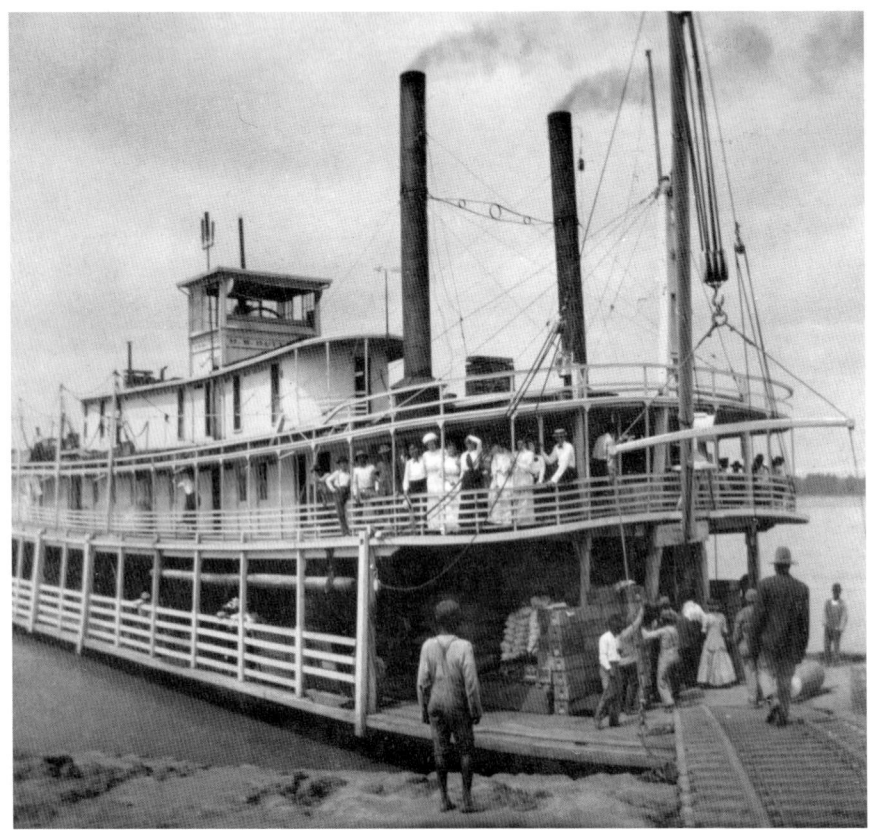

A steamboat docked in Ashport in 1938. *Tennessee State Library and Archives.*

site west of the Tennessee." The Mobile & Ohio Railroad bypassed Purdy in the 1850s; the county seat moved to Selmer in 1890.

FULTON. When it was announced, it was hard to find a fault in the Fulton business plan. "This place affords one of the best and safest steam boat landings on the Mississippi, at all seasons of the year," the December 1826 *Jackson Sun* proclaimed. Also, "the great national road from Washington City through Tennessee and onto the Arkansas Territory must of necessity pass through this place." How could it go wrong?

ASHPORT. Another Mississippi River town that couldn't miss, "the commercial advantages of Ashport are palpable to any who will examine the map of Tennessee," ads boasted in December 1836. "Its landing is perhaps the most extensive, permanent and safe in the state…therefore it is confidently expected that the survey, soon to be commenced, of the route for the great railroad through the center of the state will begin at Ashport."

RANDOLPH. A riverside community in Tipton County whose rise and fall is so interesting that it merits its own chapter (seen later in this book).

JACKSON. And what of Jackson, the town in the middle of West Tennessee that was so formidable it had a weekly newspaper by 1824? Curiously, I can't find the original ads run by the organizers of Jackson; perhaps there were none. I do know that Jackson was originally started under the name Alexandria. I also know that there was, in 1818, an attempt by two developers named Joseph and Richard Royall to start a town called Jackson in a completely different part of the state—in Middle Tennessee, on the Duck River, between Columbia and Shelbyville. That "town of Jackson" is, as best I can tell, now known as Henry Horton State Park, and the only town lots there are ones occupied by RVs on summer weekends.

SALE OF LOTS AT ASHPORT.

FROM 200 TO 400 TOWN LOTS, OF EQUAL SIZE:

WILL be sold on the premises, on Tuesday the 10th day of January, 1837, and succeeding days, on one and two years credit; other particulars of the terms made known on the day of sale:

To promote the advancement of Ashport, the proprietors bind themselves, that the proceeds of the sale of the first 200 lots, shall be invested for the completion of the Ashport Turnpike, the profits of which, and any sum that may remain of the proceeds aforesaid, shall be and remain for the use and benefit of said town, and be appropriated as the authorities of the same, when incorporated, may direct.

ASHPORT is situated on the first high land about two miles below the lower mouth of Forked Deer river, at the Foot of Canadian Reach, on the Mississippi river, in lat. 35 45, about the centre of the w stern part of the Stateof Tennessee. They outlet of Forked Deer and the back waters from the Mississippi. A levy averaging 5 feet in height, as reported by an experienced engineer who has made an actual survey, will completely shut out those waters and reclaim a large body of land, equal in soil to any in North America. The course of the levy, or Turnpike, as marked out, runs nearly parallel with the Forked Deer. Books for subscriptions to the Ashport Turnpike Stock have been opened ten days, and nearly half the amount of the same has been taken: The books for receiving subscriptions to the stock will be reopened at Ashport, Brownsville and Jackson, on the 15th inst and continue open 30 days, or until all the stock shall have been aken:

The commercial advantages of Ashport arespalpable to any who will examine the map of Tennessee. It is the nearest accessible point on the Mississippi river, to the *greatest* portion of the Western District. For all the travel from north

Nashville Republican, December 20, 1836.

A TRACE OF TRUTH

*T*he more I research Tennessee history, the more I find that granite markers and books can mislead.

I live near the northern terminus of the Natchez Trace Parkway, the limited-access highway which (allegedly) follows the route of the Natchez Trace. However, evidence indicates that this path wasn't called the Natchez Trace in the early 1800s. In fact, the actual Natchez Trace was about fifty miles to the west.

When settlers arrived in present-day Middle Tennessee around 1780, there was already a path leading southwest from there, across the Duck River in the direction of present-day Mississippi. It was first created by migrating bison but would have also been used by Native American nations such as the Chickasaw and Creek.

In 1787, in response to killings in the Nashville area, 130 men led by James Robertson took this path to the Indian village of Coldwater, where they killed about forty Creek Indians. (Coldwater is the present-day site of Tuscumbia, Alabama.) John Rains, a member of that army, referred to the route at the "Chickasaw Trace" in an 1823 interview.

In 1801, the U.S. government negotiated with the Chickasaw Nation the right to widen and use the road between present-day Middle Tennessee and Natchez, Mississippi. Under the agreement, ferries crossing rivers along this route would be the property of the Chickasaw Nation. In the treaty, the road was not referred to as the Natchez Trace, but rather as the "Columbian Highway."

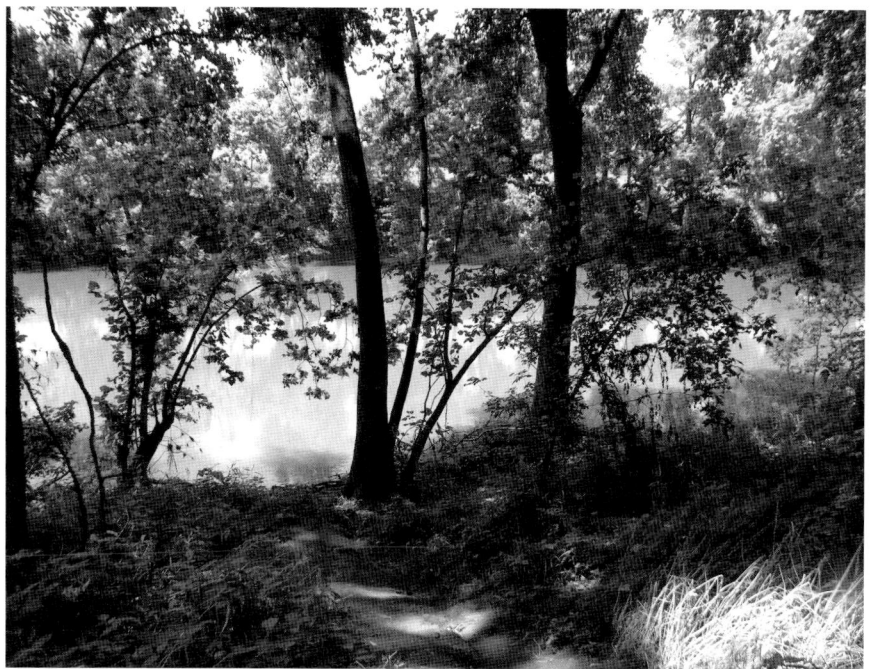

The Duck River near Gordon's Ferry. *Author's collection.*

During the next two decades, newspaper articles and ads usually referred to the route as the Chickasaw Trace, the Columbian Highway or the Natchez Road. "Charles Robinson has just opened [a] TAVERN, on Big Harpeth, 12 miles from Nashville, on the Road leading from thence to the Natchez," stated an ad in an 1801 *Tennessee Gazette.* "Accounts of the Indians on the Natchez Road are truly alarming," the *Tennessee Gazette* newspaper reported in 1803. "No company can come through without being injured and abused."

The most famous event that ever occurred along the route was the death of explorer Meriwether Lewis in present-day Lewis County, on October 11, 1809. I'll leave it to you to decide whether Lewis took his own life or was murdered. For now, I'll point out that in none of the newspaper accounts of his death was the phrase "Natchez Trace" used. It was simply reported that Lewis was staying at "the house of Mr. Grinder, near the Indian line" on a trip from New Orleans to Washington, D.C.

But what about maps? Don't they show the Natchez Trace leading from Middle Tennessee in the direction of Natchez, Mississippi? Not exactly. A 1796 map shows a road heading southwest from Nashville, crossing the

Tennessee River at a place called the "Chickasaw Crossing." Maps created in 1818, 1821, 1822, 1826 and 1831 show the same road, but none of them label it.

This brings me to Matthew Rhea's 1832 map of Tennessee—a primary source replete with remarkable and accurate detail. According to Rhea's map, the route of the present-day Natchez Trace Parkway was called the "Old Road to Nashville" through Wayne and Lawrence Counties and the "Natchez Road" in Hickman and Maury Counties. Also, in spite of it being called the "Old Road to Nashville," Rhea's map shows that the road led to Franklin, not Nashville.

Why didn't Rhea label this Middle Tennessee route the Natchez Trace? Probably because there was another road in West Tennessee that went by that name. Rhea's 1832 map shows the Natchez Trace entering Tennessee in McNairy County and then proceeding north, through Henderson, Carroll and Humphreys Counties, to the Tennessee River community of Reynoldsburg.

If you dig, you will find other primary sources that refer to this West Tennessee route as the Natchez Trace. In 1821, Nashville newspapers ran a runaway slave ad for a man last seen "thirty miles south of Reynoldsburg, near the Natchez Trace."

So much for the name controversy. What about the route? Does the current Natchez Trace Parkway follow the general route of the Natchez Road, Chickasaw Trace, Columbian Highway or whatever it was called? As best I can tell, the Natchez Trace Parkway, south of the Duck River, follows nearly (if not exactly) the actual route of the old Chickasaw Trace. But once you get north of the Duck River—into Williamson County, for instance—there have been a lot of arguments over the years.

Archaeologist William Edward Myer might have you believe the parkway is in about the right place. In his 1920 book, *Indian Trails of the Southeast*, he called the route on the west side of the Tennessee River the "West Tennessee Chickasaw Trace" and the route on the east side of the river the "Middle Tennessee Chickasaw Trace." He went on to say that the Middle Tennessee Chickasaw Trace did not go to Franklin, but rather to the western edge of Davidson County, "where there is yet a Trace Creek," he pointed out. In fact, there was, and still is, a Trace Creek. It runs close to the northern terminus of the Natchez Trace Parkway (and in the woods behind my backyard, by the way).

But a few years after Myer's book, a historian named Park Marshal wrote a long article in the *Nashville Banner*. Claiming he had researched the matter using maps, court records and interviews since 1873, Marshal said

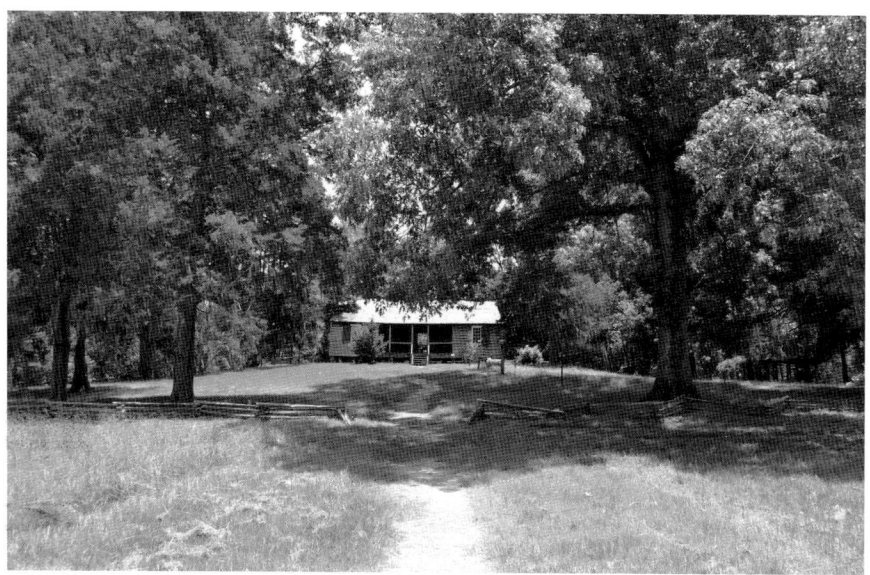

Mount Locust, in Mississippi, is said to be the oldest remaining building that contained an inn on the Natchez Trace. *Author's collection.*

the National Park Service erred when it created the northernmost parts of the Natchez Trace Parkway. "I am positively certain that is a mistake," Marshal said. He said the actual road to Natchez left Nashville along what later became known as Hillsboro Road to the Grassland community of Williamson County. It then veered right, passing near landmarks such as Robinson's Bluff, Donelson Branch, Tank Road and a "little schoolhouse" before heading in the direction of Leiper's Fork.

So here's what I've concluded: The road known in the early 1800s as the *Natchez* Trace ran west of the Tennessee River and went through present-day Natchez Trace State Park. From there it turned northeast and went to the Tennessee River port of Reynoldsburg.

The road known in the early 1800s as the *Chickasaw* Trace followed the general route of the present-day Natchez Trace Parkway. However, I'm sure the Chickasaw Trace didn't start where the Natchez Trace Parkway begins today (which is what I call "outer" Bellevue). It instead went down Hillsboro Road, to Grassland, and turned southwest along the present-day route of State Highway 46.

I'm sorry to break this to the National Park Service. And I'm sure the Natchez Trace Parkway won't be renamed the Chickasaw Trace Parkway anytime soon. But maybe it should.

BORN IN THE WAXHAWS

*I*n the process of explaining Andrew Jackson's life to eighth graders, I've come up with the following list of things that make him a fascinating man.

No one knows exactly where Andrew Jackson was born. We know he was born in an area known as the Waxhaws, along the border between North and South Carolina, and both of those states have monuments claiming his birth. One of these monuments is at Andrew Jackson State Park in South Carolina. The other is just across the state line from there, at a place where the South Carolina park ranger took me (he remained on the South Carolina side of the border while I took a photo of the North Carolina side).

Jackson's father died before he was born, and his mother and two brothers died before he was fourteen. So he had to take care of himself at a very early age, which may have had something to do with why he became such a tough young man.

Young Andrew Jackson wasn't exactly well behaved. When he was in his early twenties, he was apprenticed to a lawyer in Salisbury, North Carolina. He developed such a reputation for wildness that the citizens of Salisbury were happy to see him leave.

Andrew Jackson wasn't Rachel Jackson's first husband. When she was seventeen, she married a man named Lewis Robards. But in 1790, Robards left her, and a few months later she heard he had been granted a divorce from her. Andrew Jackson and Rachel were married the next year. But after two years of living together as man and wife, Andrew and Rachel learned that Robards had never actually been granted a divorce. Later, Lewis

Robards was granted a divorce from Rachel, and Andrew and Rachel were married again (this time legally) in 1794. What this meant is that Andrew and Rachel were living as husband and wife before they legally were husband and wife. This unintended error haunted Andrew Jackson for the rest of his life.

The first time Andrew Jackson's name appeared in a newspaper outside Tennessee (at least that I have found) was in the November 19, 1794 *Philadelphia Inquirer*. Included a long list of reports of violence in the Southwest Territory was this item: "On the 16th [of September] a woman, on Red River, near Major Sharp's, was killed by Indians— the same day a party of Indians

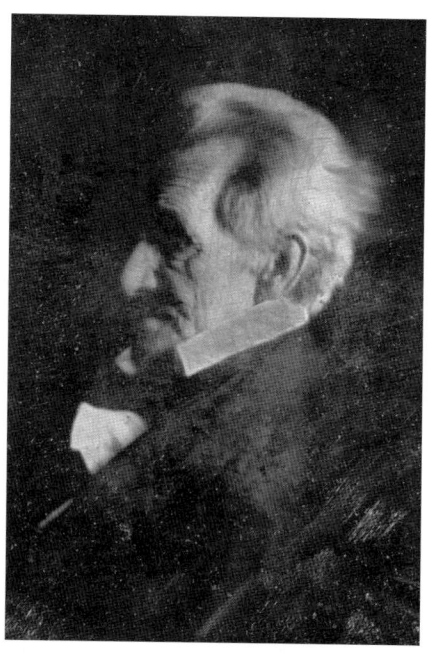

Andrew Jackson. *Library of Congress.*

fired upon five men near Mr. Andrew Jackson's, on the south side of the Cumberland River; killed one man and wounded two."

Jackson held a dim view of Native Americans in general but could be kind to them individually. During the campaign against the Creeks in 1813, his army destroyed a Creek town and killed most of the warriors they found there. But after the carnage, General Jackson found an orphaned, infant Creek, took pity on him and adopted him.

Two of the most important people in Tennessee history were Andrew Jackson and John Sevier. Naturally, they couldn't stand each other. No one is certain as to the origins of the feud, but at one point Sevier traded insults with Jackson in the streets of Knoxville. "I know of no great service you rendered the country, except taking a trip to Natchez with another man's wife," Sevier reportedly said to the future president. This exchange resulted in the two men making preparations to duel, although they never actually did so.

For most of his adult life, Jackson lived with two bullets in his body. In 1806, Jackson dueled Charles Dickinson. Dickinson died in the affair, but not before he shot Jackson in the chest. A few years later, Jackson got in a brawl with brothers Thomas and Jesse Benton in Nashville's City Hotel.

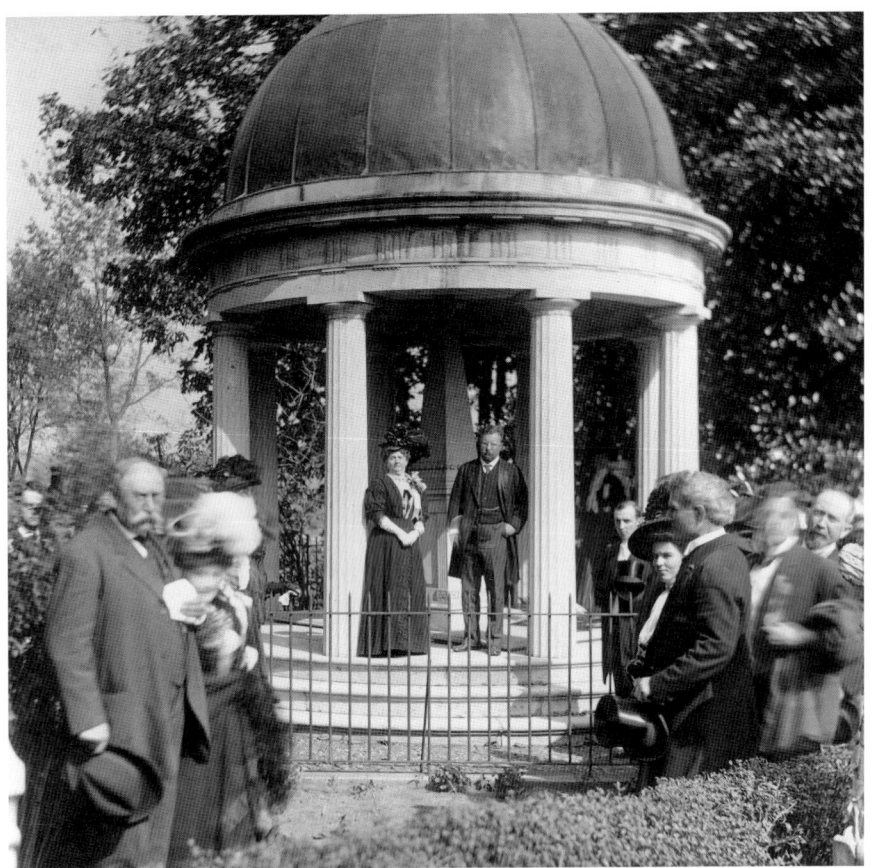

President Theodore Roosevelt visits Andrew Jackson's grave at The Hermitage. *Tennessee State Library and Archives.*

Jackson was shot twice and nearly bled to death. In spite of this violent incident, Andrew Jackson and Thomas Hart Benton became friends in the 1820s, when both were U.S. senators, and they remained political allies through Jackson's presidency.

In 1824, the first time Jackson ran for president, he won the popular vote but didn't get enough electoral votes to win. The House of Representatives settled the matter and elected John Quincy Adams president. Jackson thus became the first of two Tennesseans to run for president and win the popular vote but lose the election. The second, of course, was Al Gore in 2000.

When Jackson was president, the State of South Carolina threatened to secede from the Union because people there were opposed to a tariff. Jackson was furious and made it clear that if South Carolina tried to secede, the U.S. government would wage war against it. "In forty days I can have within the limits of South Carolina fifty thousand men, and in forty days another fifty thousand," he wrote at the time.

South Carolina backed down. But twenty-eight years later, the same state tried to leave the Union again. Another American president, Abraham Lincoln, reacted in much the way Jackson intended to. This time, however, South Carolina didn't back down, and the result was the Civil War.

WITHOUT ANY JUST CAUSE

I've heard it said that families were happier "in the old days." However, newspapers prove that not every household was blissful. They also remind us that when it comes to legal status, women have come a long way.

There were several types of runaway ads published during Tennessee's antebellum era. There were runaway horse ads. During periods of military activity (such as the early wars against Native Americans), there were deserter ads, offering rewards for the return of a soldier who abandoned his military unit. At a time when it was a big part of Tennessee's economy, there were runaway indentured servant ads. There were, I'm sorry to say, runaway slave ads (in fact, I wrote an entire book about Tennessee's runaway slave ads called *Runaways, Coffles and Fancy Girls*).

None of these have taken me by surprise. But the "runaway wife" ads have. A typical one can be found in the November 9, 1805 *Mero District Advertiser*. "I do hereby forewarn all persons from crediting my wife Polly Cartwright, on my account, or harboring her, as she has left my bed and board without any just cause," the ad states. "I am therefore determined to pay no debts of her contracting, and will prosecute any person harboring her, with the utmost rigor of the Law. Robert Cartwright."

I've found similar ads published by John Smith of Knox County regarding his wife, Margaret (1792); Isaac Sanders of Robertson County regarding his wife, Elizabeth (1814); Richard Crunk of Dickson County regarding his wife, Mary (1825); Zebulon Hassell of Hickman County regarding his wife,

Unity (1836); James Bland of Lincoln County regarding his wife, Permalia (1857); and the list goes on and on.

The wording of these ads is generally the same: The husband claims his wife has left his "bed and board," usually "without any just cause." The husband warns merchants from "trading with or crediting her" on his account, saying he will pay none of her debts from this day forward.

The purpose of this chapter is not to air out centuries-old marital discord, but rather to make a point about life on the American frontier. We can talk all we want about how much women contributed to the household and to society in early frontier history. Legally, however, women were second-class citizens. A woman who left her husband did have more legal rights than a runaway slave or indentured servant. (She wasn't thrown in jail, for instance.) But a runaway wife didn't have the same rights as her husband. "Married women generally were not allowed to make contracts, devise wills, take part in other legal transactions, or control any wages they might earn," explained Tim Crumrin, who was a longtime historian for the Conner Prairie living history museum in Indiana. "One of the few legal advantages of marriage for a woman was that her husband was obligated to support her and be responsible for her debts."

The frequency of "runaway wife" ads also reminds us that the frontier economy didn't run on cash. Local merchants extended credit to everyone and collected monthly or even seasonally. These runaway wife ads may, to us, simply appear to be an attempt by a jealous husband to shame his wife. But they were also the frontier equivalent of canceling the credit card.

At a time when all the assets of a marriage were considered the property of the husband, and at a time when most occupations were closed to women, the implications of such ads were clear. In the old days, a wife who left her husband needed financial help from someone else.

This all may sound rather harsh. However, runaway wife ads became so common in Tennessee that the November 8, 1850 *Athens Post* made light of them with the following poem:

> *Eunice, my wife, has grown quite lewd,*
> *And left me in a lonesome mood,*
> *She's gone in spite of friends and church.*
> *And went to live with Timothy Murch.*
> *She left my board, and took my bed,*
> *She carried off my meat and bread,*
> *Know you, therefore, who read this paper,*

That since she has cut this reckless caper,
I will not pay a single fraction
For any debts of her contraction.

If this chapter hasn't offended you yet, keep reading. At a time when West Tennessee was *the* frontier, it was difficult for the first wave of settlers to find available ladies. In any case, here is an advertisement in the June 12, 1824 *Jackson Gazette*:

> *$2000!!! WANTED IMMEDIATELY, a YOUNG LADY, of the following description* [as a wife]*—with about $2000 as a patrimony, sweet temper, spend but little, be a good house-wife, and reasonably handsome.—And as I am under 30 years of age, I hope it will not be difficult to find a good wife. A letter addressed to "A.B." and left at the Post-Office will be attended to.*

We don't know if "A.B." was serious; we don't know if he meant it as a joke. We also don't know if anyone ever responded to his advertisement. But we do know, or at least I hope we do, that times have changed.

SWAN CREEK, UGLY CREEK

*D*o you like maps? I always have, and my son thinks there's something wrong with me because I like maps so much. I've been known to download maps on the internet and stare, shaking my head in amazement at how much information can be gleaned from them. "Dad, are you still looking at that map?" he's been known to ask.

My favorite Tennessee map was produced in 1832 by the cartographer Matthew Rhea. Three years in the making, Rhea's map was a detailed work of art originally about nine feet long and three feet high. That's why its digital file (which can be downloaded at both the Tennessee State Library and Archives and U.S. Library of Congress) is so massive.

I've done entire inservices on Rhea's map, showing parts of it on power point slides that amaze teachers (at least I think they are amazed; maybe they are sarcastic oohs and aahs). I can't be quite so visual in this chapter, but Rhea's map is full of fascinating tidbits I can mention here.

Rhea did a wonderful job showing the locations of creeks. Pigeon Roost Creek in Giles County makes it, as does Bat Creek in Monroe County and Cyprus Creek in Dyer County. I count fifteen creeks in Hickman County alone—from the wonderfully named Swan Creek to its tributary Ugly Creek.

Quite a few county seats have moved, while many of the county seats in 1832 are now abandoned. Examples include Monroe (Overton County), Montgomery (Morgan County), Reynoldsburg (Humphries County) and Perryville (Perry County).

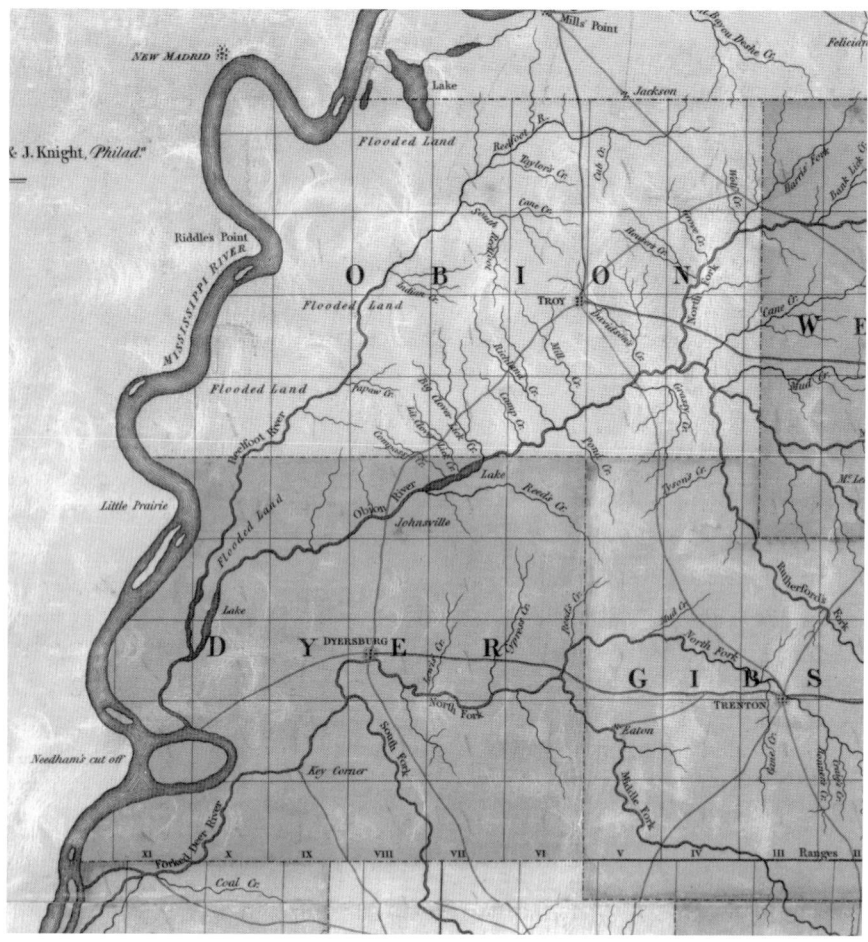

The northwest corner of Tennessee as shown in Matthew Rhea's 1832 map. *Library of Congress.*

Speaking of courthouses that have moved: In the southwestern corner of the state, you can clearly see that Raleigh, not Memphis, was the county seat of Shelby County. It would remain so until after the Civil War, when a new courthouse was built in Memphis and all the paperwork moved from Raleigh to there.

Reelfoot Lake, formed by the New Madrid earthquakes of 1811–12, is not shown on Rhea's map—apparently because no one was sure it was permanent. The only indication that there is something unusual about the terrain in the northwest part of Tennessee is the use of the phrase "flooded land" four times over parts of Obion and Dyer Counties.

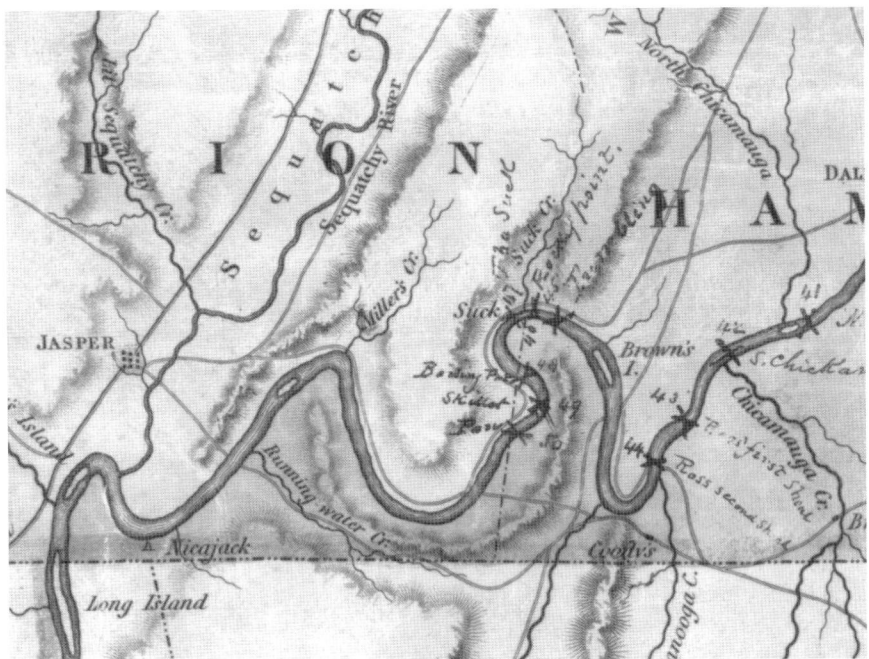

The Tennessee River downstream from Chattanooga as shown in Rhea's 1832 map. *Library of Congress.*

At the opposite end of the state, the shape of northeast Tennessee looks familiar on Rhea's map, but that's about all that is recognizable. Johnson City and Bristol aren't shown because they didn't exist yet, while Kingsport looks pretty small. The important communities in northeast Tennessee were still Elizabethton, Blountville, Jonesborough, Greeneville and Rogersville, and they would remain so for quite some time.

On Rhea's map, the only Nashville feature that made the map is the state penitentiary. In 1832, in Matthew Rhea's opinion, the most important thing in Nashville was a prison.

I was surprised by the number of Indian mounds and colonial-era ruins on Rhea's map. The site of Fort Loudon (destroyed in the 1750s) is mapped, as is Stone Fort (now known as Old Stone Fort) and "Mound Pinson" (now known as Pinson Mounds). Near the border between Rutherford and Bedford Counties, his map shows "Old Fort Nash," a structure which, as best I can tell, was occupied only for about five years in the early 1790s. (This is especially interesting because no one living today knows exactly where Fort Nash was—it's one of those structures whose location was lost to history.)

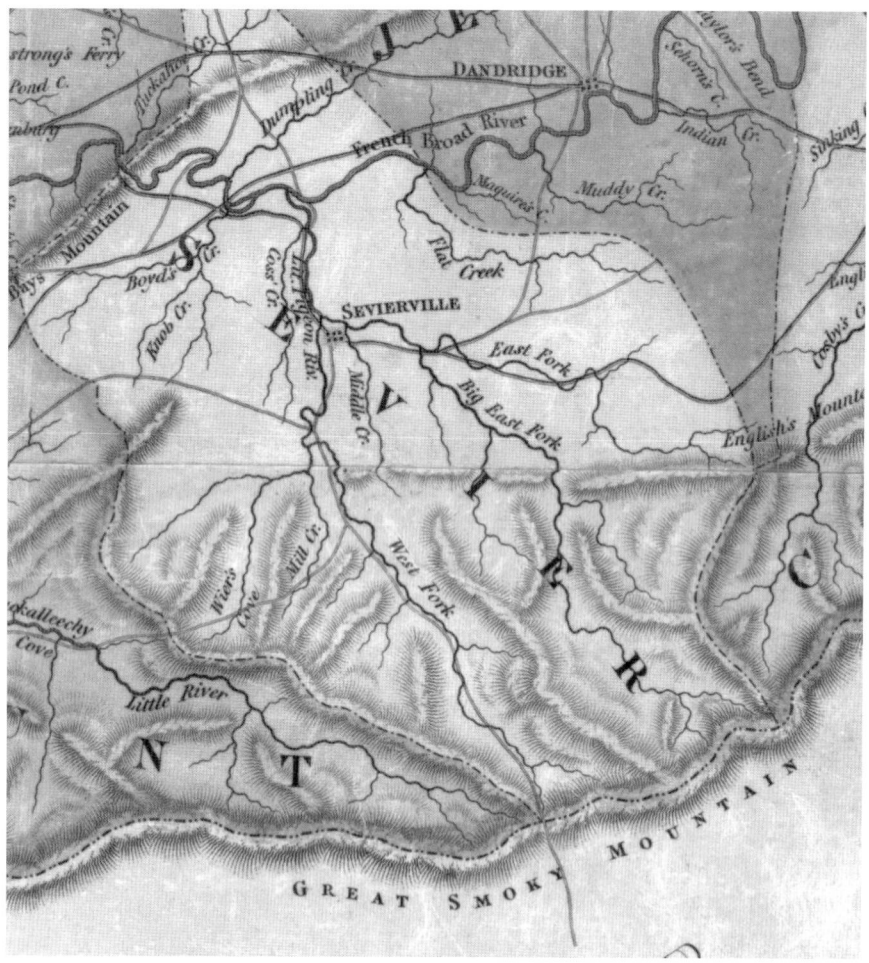

Sevier County as shown in Rhea's 1832 map. *Library of Congress.*

Speaking of odd things on the map, only a single grave makes it— Meriwether Lewis's grave at the junction of Hickman, Maury and Lawrence Counties.

One of the versions of Rhea's map you can find online has handwritten markings on it. Apparently, someone who owned the map in the 1830s wrote the location of every obstacle along the Tennessee River, starting in Knoxville. According to the map, there were more than fifty such places, and the person who wrote on the map named most of them for people who lived nearby (or maybe the person who operated the nearby ferry— I'm not sure). Rhea County had seven navigational obstacles (Gillespie's,

Walton's, Well's, Kelly's, Lea's, Hiwassee and one I can't make out). Just downstream from present-day Chattanooga, this person noted the exact locations of well-known Tennessee River obstacles such as the Suck, the Boiling Pot and the Skillet.

There are parts of Tennessee that today have towns and cities in them that had no towns or cities in 1832. Places in and near the Cumberland Plateau such as Tullahoma, Monteagle, Cookeville and Crossville didn't exist yet. The same can be said for East Tennessee communities such as Pigeon Forge and Gatlinburg. As you see the open space on the map, it does make you wonder what the mountains and valleys looked like in the early nineteenth century.

The map shows the locations of mills and forges throughout the state, but some counties get more coverage in this regard than others. Rhea showed ten mills in Hardeman County, but only one in McNairy County and none in Henderson County. Meanwhile, sixteen Carter County forges made Rhea's map!

Since it didn't exist in 1832, the city of Chattanooga didn't make Rhea's map. In fact, the only towns mapped along the Tennessee River, south of Kingston, are Washington (in Rhea County), Dallas (in Hamilton County) and the Chickamaugan village of Nickajack. Today, none of these communities remains.

Speaking of the Hamilton County community of Dallas, since it appeared on Rhea's map, we know Dallas, Tennessee, predated Dallas, Texas. The next time you meet a swaggering Texan, point out that his state stole the name "Dallas" from Tennessee. I'm sure that will go over well.

LETTERS ETCHED IN STONE

*T*here are abandoned iron furnaces all over Dickson, Stewart and Montgomery Counties—limestone monoliths ranging from thirty to fifty feet high that cause passersby to stop and stare.

One of them is the Bear Spring Furnace, just east of Dover. It sits in a rural part of a county in which, today, only about 1 percent of the residents are African American. And yet, in October 1834, because of the death of Thomas Yeatman, the entire industrial operation at Bear Spring Furnace was set to be auctioned—forge, factory, horses, wagons, eighteen thousand acres and no fewer than two hundred enslaved people.

For years I've wondered who Yeatman was and how why the only thing left of him is a few letters etched in stone. In 1815, Yeatman ran a Nashville dry goods store that sold everything from cloth to spices to glassware—things people wanted but had to import from far away. Like every other merchant of that era, he operated on credit. In the fall, after harvest season, he'd ask his customers to settle their accounts. Then he'd make the long trip to Philadelphia, where he'd order all the goods he intended to stock the next year. "Those persons indebted to the subscriber will please call at his store to settle their accounts, as he expects to start for Philadelphia in a few weeks," he announced in a *Nashville Whig* ad in November 1816.

Yeatman made this trip every winter, making better contacts with merchants and bankers each time. On one of his buying trips, he learned there had been a sharp increase in the price of cotton. Yeatman sped home from Philadelphia, moving faster than the U.S. mail en route. (Remember, the telegraph did not exist yet.) Once he got home, he bought up all the

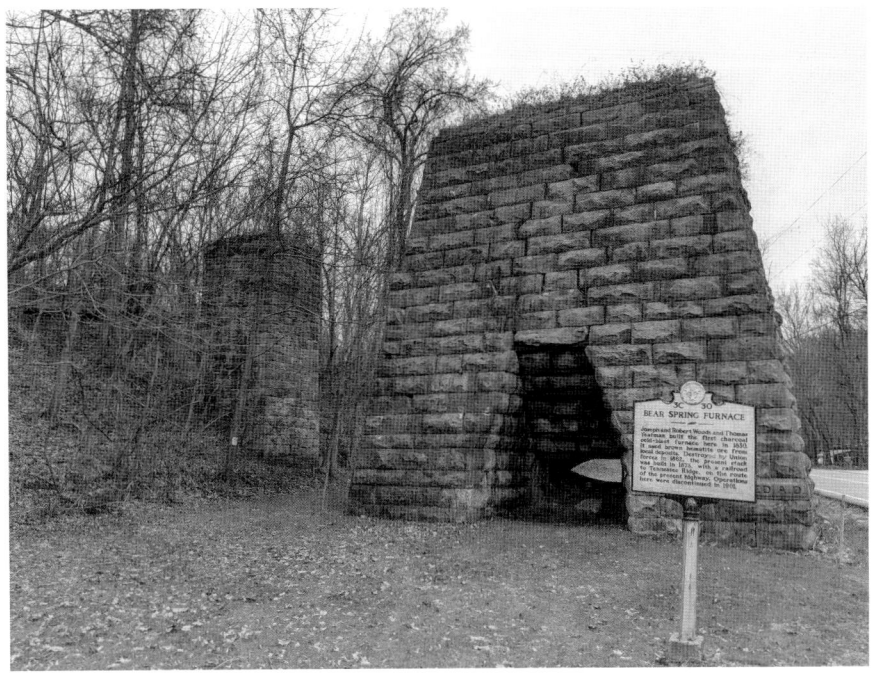

The Bear Spring Furnace. *Author's collection.*

cotton he could find in the warehouses of Middle Tennessee and North Alabama at twelve and a half cents per pound, knowing it would be worth twenty-five cents per pound when it got to distant markets.

Yeatman made a lot of money on the cotton deal, but he didn't stop there. He built a large warehouse beside the Cumberland River in Nashville, where tobacco and cotton were stored before being loaded onto boats. He partnered with Joseph and Robert Woods and bought a steamboat, then second and then a third, called the *Thomas Yeatman*.

In 1825, the partners started a bank—Yeatman Woods & Company— which would remain one of the best-known financial institutions in the South for decades. (If you do a Google search, you'll find images of its currency from the early nineteenth century.)

Thomas Yeatman loaned money for many ventures, ranging from the Franklin Turnpike Company to the Nashville Water Works. He bought and sold paper currency. Although he was not a professional slave trader, he was a slaveholder who loaned money to other slaveholders so they could buy more slaves. His three steamboats would have been regularly commissioned to move enslaved people west as part of the interstate slave

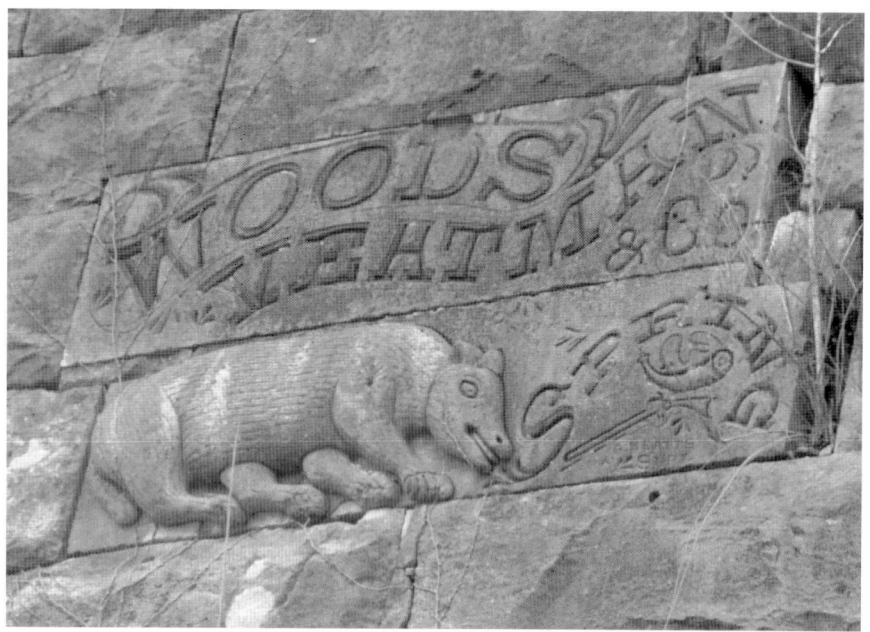

The words "Woods, Yeatman & Co." are etched on a stone at the Bear Spring Furnace. *Author's collection.*

trade. In fact, an explosion on board the *Thomas Yeatman* killed half a dozen enslaved men in 1833. The *Thomas Yeatman* was also one of the steamboats hired by the U.S. government to move Cherokee and Choctaw Indians west during the Trail of Tears.

In the early 1800s, the most important industry on the Highland Rim was iron—separating ore into pig iron and then shaping it into nails, horseshoes, kitchen appliances, wagon axles and other products. These iron furnaces required thousands of acres and hundreds of people to tend fires and haul rock, firewood and finished product. It was difficult, hot work, and a lot of it was done by enslaved people.

In 1830, Yeatman Woods & Company purchased Dickson County's Cumberland Iron Works. The firm then built another big operation in Stewart County, east of Dover. In 1833, Bear Spring Furnace, led by Yeatman Woods & Company partner Joseph Woods, produced two thousand tons of rolled iron and four thousand kegs of nails.

But on June 12, 1833, at the age of forty-five, Thomas Yeatman died of cholera on a steamboat bound for Philadelphia. The legal process of settling his estate led to plans being made for the Bear Spring operation to be auctioned in October 1834.

CHANCERY SALE.

IN virtue of a decree of the Court of Chancery of the Western Division of Tennessee, the ndersigned commisioner appointed by said Court, ill expose to public sale, on *Thursday the 2nd day* of *Oct. next*, all the property, real personal and mixd, of Yeatman, Woods & Co. in Stewart county, State of Tennessee.

The real property consists of about 18,000 acres of LAND, on both sides of Cumberland river, on which is erected one large ROLLING MILL, immediately on the south bank of said river, with a steam engine estimated at 120 horse power. The Rolling Mill is now in complete operation, making iron of every description, on a large scale Attached to said mill is a NAILERY with five machines for making nails.

Also—one STEAM BLAST FURNACE about one mile from the Rolling mill called "Bear Spring Furnace," now in complete opperation, manufacturing Pig metal. A FORGE attached, with a nobling hammer for the manufacture of Bloon Iron.

Also—one other STEAM BLAST FURNACE, about 4 miles from the Rolling mill, called ' Dover Furnace," now in complete operation, manufacturing Pig metal and castings of all kind. There is attached to the Rolling mill and Furnaces, all the necessary dwelling houses, negroe houses, work shops, and stabling for such establishments.

There will also be included in said sale, TWO HUNDRED SLAVES, among which are Engineers Forgemen, Hammermen, and Workmen of almost every description required at such establishments.— Also, all the stock of horses, mules, oxens, wagons and gears, carts, implements and tools for digging ore for coaling, &c. &c. Also—all the household and kitchen furniture, milch cows. &c. &c. on hand on the day of sale, at Said Rolling mill and Furnace. Also, one keel boat, and two Tow boats.

The sale will take place on the day above named, at the "Rolling mill." The terms, as prescribed by the Chancellor, CASH.

The death of Thomas Yeatman having rendered the sale of the foregoing property necessary to make a proper distribution between his heirs and surviving partners, the sale will therefore be peremptory; and upon the ratification thereof by the Chancellor and payment of the purchase money, titles will be made.

E. S. HALL, *Commissioner.*

Nashville Republican, August 19, 1834.

As it turns out, outsiders did not take over ownership of the Bear Spring Furnace; Yeatman's sons and remaining partners simply shifted their ownership percentages. In 1843, the firm expanded and changed its name to Woods, Yeatman & Company. By the time the Civil War began, the business owned nearly sixty thousand acres and enslaved more than four hundred people.

The U.S. Army destroyed much of the iron smelting operation in the weeks after the Battle of Fort Donelson in 1862, but the owners rebuilt the operation after the war and built the limestone forge still standing on Highway 49 in Stewart County. But in the late 1870s, a sharp decline in iron prices soured the outlook for the industry. In 1878, the business sold fourteen thousand acres, and it was never the same after that.

Reading the complicated story of Yeatman, Woods and the Bear Spring Furnace might make you overlook that each of the enslaved people who showed up on the company balance sheets was a human being. But here's a troubling anecdote from the history of the Highland Rim: In 1856, there was a rebellion among the thousands of enslaved people who worked in the iron industry in Montgomery, Dickson and Stewart Counties. Although the extent of the insurrection was probably exaggerated in the press (as such rebellions typically were in that era), six of the enslaved were executed for their alleged roles in the insurrection.

Among the condemned were some of the enslaved held by U.S. Senator John Bell of Tennessee. Bell had acquired those slaves two decades earlier, when he married Thomas Yeatman's widow, Jane Eakin Yeatman.

FOUR DAYS FROM NASHVILLE TO KNOXVILLE

Before the airplane, car, railroad and steamboat, there was the stagecoach. From the 1790s until the 1850s, horse-drawn stagecoaches were the most common way to get from one part of Tennessee to another. Like buses, trains and airplanes, stagecoaches had scheduled routes and stops. Stops evolved into inns, where people could eat and rest and where the coach would get a fresh set of horses.

Early stagecoach operators also carried the mail. This partnering of U.S. mail with passenger service meant coaches didn't always take the direct route. It also meant people would share the ride with bags of letters, boxes and even furniture.

By all accounts, stagecoach travel was unpleasant and uncomfortable. Traveling around five miles an hour, trips that take three hours by car today might have taken three days by stagecoach in 1840. Passengers were packed into tiny spaces, bouncing along rocky, unpaved roads, which were muddy in the winter and spring and dusty in the summer and fall.

What happened when passengers had to use the bathroom? What happened when they got sick along the way? Best not think about it.

Stagecoach travel could also be dangerous, especially when going up and down mountains or crossing flooded rivers. In 1823, a stagecoach tried to cross flooded Mill Creek in Nashville when one of the horses fell and was drowned. Driver, passengers and cargo were washed downstream for about half a mile, when fourteen-year-old William Osmar jumped in

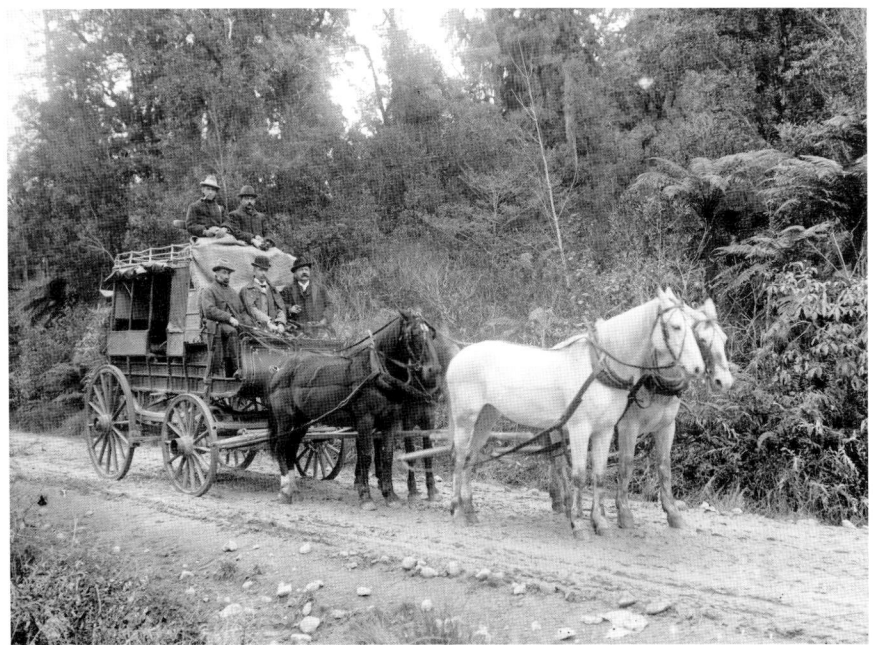

A stagecoach. *Library of Congress.*

and saved both the driver and the mail bags. The *Nashville Whig* was so impressed with the young man's courage and fortitude that it started a fund to give money to the lad—an early version of a GoFundMe account, I suppose. As for the grown men who stood by and did nothing, the paper said "their names should be known, that they might be held up to public scorn, the just reward of such heartless conduct."

Tennessee's first stagecoach road went from Abingdon, Virginia, to Knoxville, via Blountville, Kingsport, Rogersville and Rutledge. Most of East Tennessee's early settlers migrated to Tennessee on this road. Stagecoaches that traveled along it brought furniture, packages, newspapers and other commodities to and from Knoxville. Today, some of these stagecoach inns are still standing, such as Blountville's Old Deery Inn, Kingsport's Netherland Inn and Rogersville's Hale Springs Inn.

When settlers first migrated to Middle Tennessee in the 1780s, there wasn't much of a road across the Cumberland Plateau, which was still Cherokee territory. Families who migrated west took flatboats down the Tennessee River or traveled by land to Kingston, where they waited for soldiers to escort them across the plateau. By the mid-1790s, there was a safe, decent road across the Cumberland Plateau (at least by standards of

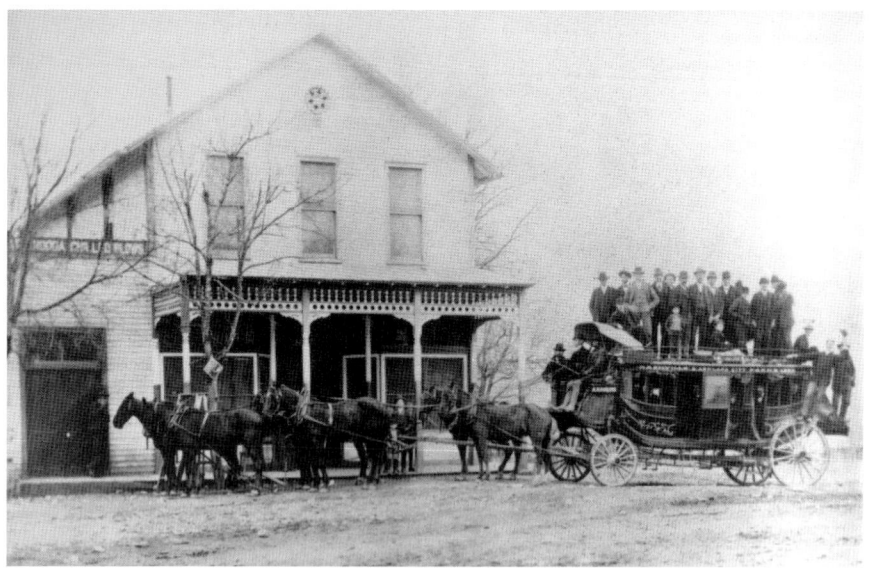

This photo of the Nashville and Ashland City stagecoach (taken around 1880) shows how crowded stagecoach travel could be. *Tennessee State Library and Archives.*

the time). This road became a stagecoach thoroughfare, with stops along the way such as Rock House, near Sparta (a structure still standing).

From newspaper ads, here are some other points I've learned about the evolution of Tennessee's stagecoach routes:

In 1817, it took nearly four days to get from Nashville to Knoxville. The stagecoach left Nashville Friday afternoon at 1:00 p.m. and arrived in Knoxville, Tuesday at 10:00 a.m.

It took about twenty-one hours to get from Nashville to McMinnville in 1824. The stagecoach left Nashville three times a week, departing at 1:00 p.m. and arriving in McMinnville the next morning.

In 1829, Knoxville had a weekly stagecoach to Huntsville, Alabama. The journey took twenty-two hours and passed through Maryville, Tellico, Athens, Washington (in Rhea County, where it crossed the Tennessee River), Pikeville, Jasper and Bellefont (Alabama).

Another coach left Knoxville twice a week, heading northeast, through Dandridge, Newport, Greeneville, Jonesborough, Elizabethton and Shown's Crossroads (near present-day Mountain City). From there, passengers could take a different coach to points farther away such as Washington, D.C.

There was a thrice-weekly mail coach between Nashville and Memphis in 1830. Leaving Nashville at 1:00 a.m., it passed through Charlotte, Reynoldsburg (in Humphreys County), Huntington, Jackson, Bolivar, Sommerville and Raleigh—arriving in Memphis three and a half days later. This middle-of-the-night departure time wasn't unheard of; in 1846, a daily stagecoach left Nashville for Columbia at 1:00 a.m.

In 1833, Robert Jetton claimed his coaches made it all the way from Nashville to Huntsville on the same day (passing through Murfreesboro, Shelbyville and Fayetteville en route).

The city of Chattanooga was not officially named until 1839. I was therefore interested to see that, a year before it was named, a stagecoach route from Murfreesboro to Athens, Georgia, passed through "Chatanooga"—spelled with one *t*. R.A. Ramsey, the owner of the coach, said Chatanooga was "destined shortly to be the greet emporium of East Tennessee." This may have been the first time the name of Tennessee's fourth-largest city ever appeared in newspapers.

Five years later, the operators of the Knoxville–Nashville route said that their coach could make the trip in only fifty hours. They further boasted that their stagecoaches were made in Troy, New York, which was then known for making great stagecoaches. "The accommodations on the road are believed to be better than they ever were before, and are the best which can be procured," the ads claimed.

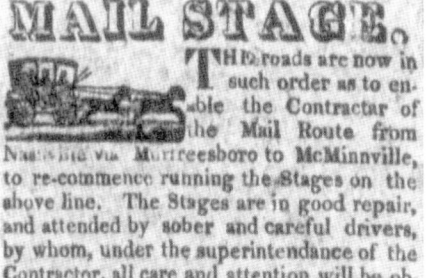

Left: *Nashville Whig*, April 26, 1824. *Right*: *Knoxville Register*, May 29, 1829.

In 1850, the Southwestern Stage Station in Nashville was the closest thing to Grand Central Station Tennessee had at the time. Coaches left as early as 4:00 a.m. and as late as 8:00 p.m., with regular service to Memphis, Louisville, Knoxville, Chattanooga, Huntsville and Tuscumbia.

It was about then that railroads came to Tennessee, reducing dramatically the time it took to travel from one place to another and wiping out most coach line services in the process. While railroads were being built, there were times when long journeys required multiple legs. Rather than "plane, train and automobile," these journeys would be better described as "train, steamboat and stagecoach." In 1853, the journey from Nashville to Memphis was, shall we say, quite the adventure. First you took a train from Nashville to Chattanooga. Then you boarded a steamboat that took you from Chattanooga to Tuscumbia—the boat dodging barriers to navigation such as the Suck and the Boiling Pot en route. Then you took a stagecoach from Tuscumbia to LaGrange. Then you took the train from LaGrange to Memphis. All this for only $15 (the equivalent of $576 adjusted for inflation)!

The arrival of the railroads spelled the end of the professional, long-distance stagecoach business. But there was another level of horse-drawn conveyance that would remain a part of Tennessee's culture for about another half century. Known as the "mail hack," it delivered mail and passengers from train stations to small communities. Horse-drawn mail hacks to towns such as Mountain City, Sevierville, Lynchburg and Whiteville would remain until around 1920, when the U.S. postal service upgraded to automobiles.

MANACLED AND CHAINED

*T*ennessee's newspapers are full of ads documenting the sale of an enslaved person from one slaveholder to another. They do not, however, reveal much about how slaves got from places such as Virginia and North Carolina to Tennessee, nor do they tell us much about how those same people were forced to migrate to places even farther south and west such as Mississippi and Louisiana. The saga of a Tennessee-born slave trader named Isaac Franklin does, however, tell us about this larger story.

James Franklin first came to Middle Tennessee in the 1770s. By the early 1800s, he had a plantation in the Station Camp Creek area, north of the Cumberland River in what eventually became Sumner County. James Franklin had ten children. As a teenager, son Isaac would have gone with his father on the annual river trips to New Orleans, where products from the farm were sold and traded. Isaac thus became familiar with rafting on the Cumberland and the Mississippi, trading in New Orleans and traveling the long road from Natchez to Nashville.

Between 1770 and 1810, Middle Tennessee was America's western frontier. But after about 1820, Americans migrated farther south and west into present-day West Tennessee, Arkansas, Mississippi and Louisiana. At the time, this region of the country was an unbroken forest inhabited by bears and other beasts of prey, as described by early settlers such as David Crockett.

As settlers moved into these areas, they began to clear the land and plant cotton and sugar. This took manpower, which meant enslaved people. However, the large slave populations were in states such as Virginia, North

We will give Cash

FOR one hundred likely YOUNG NEGROES of both sexes, between the ages of 8 and 25 years. Persons who wish to sell, would do well to give us a call, as the negros are wanted immediately We will give more than any other purchasers that are in market or may hereafter come into market.

Any letters addressed to the subscribers through the Post Office at Alexandria, will be promptly attended to. For information, enquire at the subscribers', west end of Duke-street, Alexandria, D. C.

nov 11   FRANKLIN & ARMFIELD

Left: Alexandria *Phenix Gazette*, December 4, 1828.

Opposite: The building that had previously been the headquarters of Franklin & Armfield in Alexandria, Virginia, shown during the Civil War. *Library of Congress.*

Carolina and Maryland. These Atlantic states had a glut of slaves because tobacco had declined as a cash crop and because such populations had risen due to natural increases (birth rates exceeding death rates).

By 1800, slaves cost twice as much money in New Orleans as in Richmond. Virginia planters were aware of this disparity in value. This was the main reason Thomas Jefferson and other prominent Virginia farmers were in favor of the ban on the importation of slaves to the United States (which went into effect in 1808).

We know Isaac Franklin was selling slaves in Natchez in 1819—probably ones he bought in Tennessee and took there on log rafts. In 1828, Franklin started a long-distance slave trading firm with his nephew John Armfield. With business associates operating throughout Virginia and Maryland, Franklin & Armfield bought slaves from tobacco plantations in the east and transported them to New Orleans and Natchez, where they were sold at great profit. According to 1828 advertisements in the (Alexandria) *Phenix Gazette* and the *Washington Daily National Intelligencer*, Franklin & Armfield was in the market for 150 slaves. Thanks to increasing lines of credit from various banks, that number soon grew to 500.

As plantations sold slaves to Franklin and Armfield, the company would at first house them in so-called slave pens, the best known of which was adjacent to the firm's building in Alexandria. Slaves might live there for days or weeks, milling around the outdoor prison during the day and sleeping in a two-story adjacent building while chained up at night. Once enough people had been accumulated, the company would usually transport them to New Orleans by ship. Early on, Franklin & Armfield sent slaves via third-party liners. As the business got bigger, it purchased its own ship, then another, then another, until by 1832 the company owned at least four.

Because of the legal requirement that maritime manifests contain passenger lists, we have a lot of data about how many slaves the company

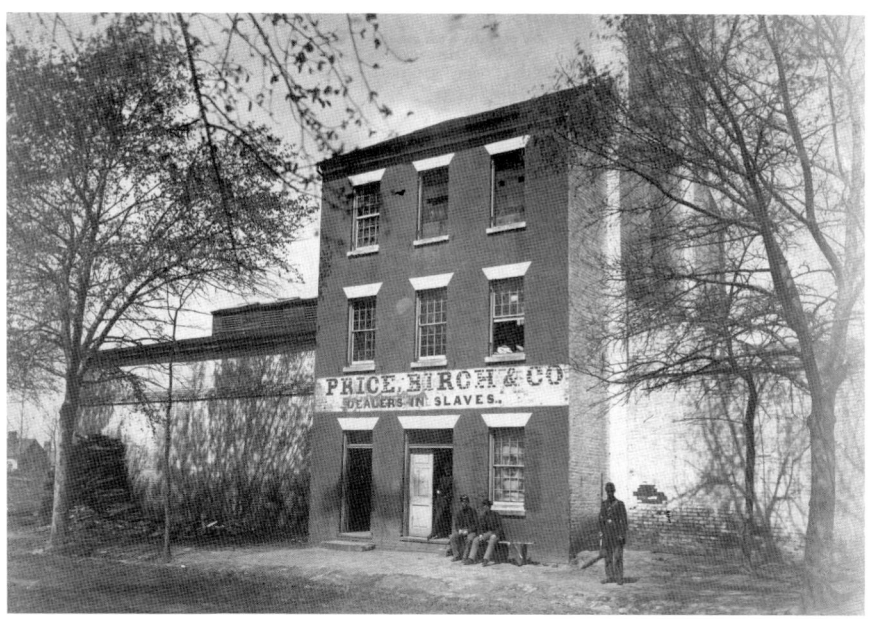

transported to New Orleans. The shipping season for slave transport ran from October through May, and at its peak, Franklin & Armfield would send about seventy-five to one hundred slaves per trip and as many as two boats per month on the long journey around the Florida Panhandle. On the return voyage to Virginia, the ships carried passengers, sugar, molasses, whiskey and cotton.

In the summer, the company would move slaves by land, herding as many as three hundred people per trip in slave caravans known as coffles. These overland trips would come right across Tennessee, through Blountville, Knoxville and Kingston and then over the Cumberland Plateau to Nashville—following the general route later taken by Highway 70. From there, slaves would either be loaded onto boats and floated downriver or marched down the road to Natchez and sold at the slave market known as the Forks in the Road.

Slave coffles were a common sight in the South—so common, in fact, that it wasn't even news when they passed through towns. However, northerners and Europeans who visited the South were often shocked when they stumbled on these forced marches.

One was G.W. Featherstonhaugh, an English geologist who encountered a Franklin & Armfield coffle in southwest Virginia in September 1834. "It was a camp of negro slave-drivers, just packing up to start; they had about three hundred slaves with them, who had bivouacked the preceding night in chains in the woods," he wrote. Featherstonhaugh noted that the caravan included nine wagons to carry supplies and to transport any slaves who could not walk. Describing what he saw, he said "the female slaves were, some of them, sitting on logs of wood, whilst others were standing, and a great many little black children were warming themselves at the fires of the bivouac. In front of them all, and prepared for the march, stood, in double files, about two hundred male slaves, manacled and chained to each other."

Another account of a slave coffle came from a northern visitor to Virginia named William Seward, who was visiting a country tavern in Virginia when he saw something he never forgot. "Ten naked little boys, between six and twelve years old, tied together, two and two, by their wrists, were all fastened to a long rope," Seward wrote. They were "followed by a tall, gaunt white man who, with his long lash, whipped up the sad and weary procession, drove it to the horse-trough to drink, and thence to a shed, where they lay down on the ground and sobbed and moaned themselves to sleep....These were children gathered up at different plantations by the 'trader,' and were to be driven down to Richmond to be sold at auction, and taken South."

Seward never knew which firm's employee or agent he saw driving the naked children that day. But the sight of the sad procession was one of many things that turned him against slavery. Seward later became New York governor, senator and U.S. secretary of state in the Lincoln and Johnson administrations. However, he is best remembered today for something which has nothing to do with slavery; it was when he was secretary of state that the U.S. government acquired Alaska from Russia—thus the nickname "Seward's Folly" for the forty-ninth state.

Why Franklin & Armfield transported slaves via both land and sea, rather than just via one method, is something we aren't sure of today. A 1938 biography of Isaac Franklin maintains that the sea route was quicker but more expensive and more dangerous because it didn't give the slaves time to acclimate to the Louisiana climate.

Another idea of why slave traders such as Franklin & Armfield might have chosen the overland route over the sea route can be derived from the 1848 autobiography of former slave Henry Watson. Watson recalled being sold to a Richmond trader named Denton, who chained his slaves together and forced the coffle to march all the way to Natchez. "I will not weary my readers with the particulars of our march to Tennessee, where we stopped several days for the purpose of arranging our clothes," Watson recalled. "While stopping, the men were hired out to pick cotton." Watson's

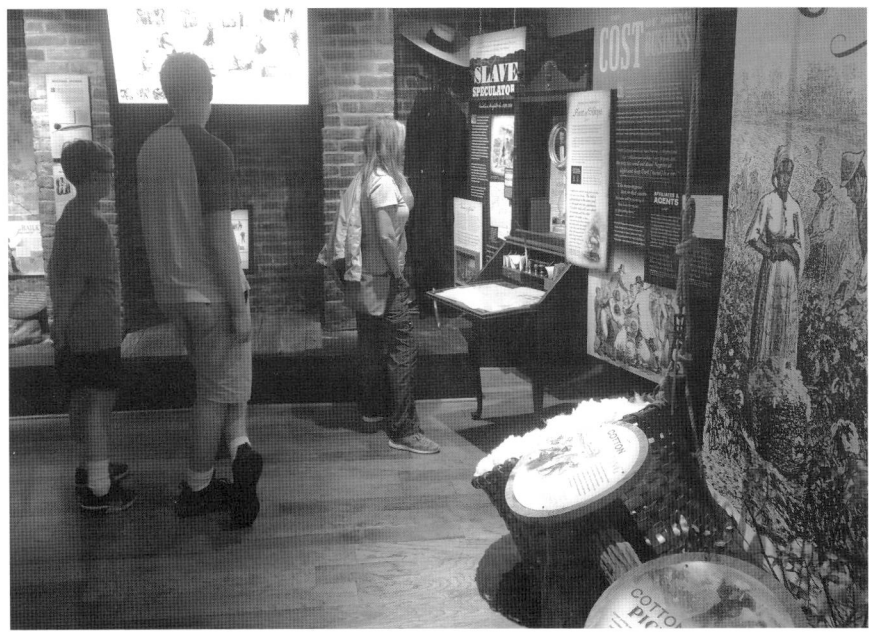

Franklin & Armfield's headquarters in Alexandria is now the Freedom House Museum. *Author's collection.*

recollection raises the possibility that Isaac Franklin might have used his Sumner County plantation as a stopover on the journey. This would have allowed him the added benefit of using the slaves he was transporting to harvest crops at his Tennessee plantation.

Because it was so large, because it involved the movement of so many people and because we have so many records of it, Franklin & Armfield is the best-documented slave trading firm in American history. It also may have been the largest. From 1828 until 1836, the firm bought, moved and sold an estimated 1,000 to 1,200 slaves per year, making it responsible for the forced migration of more than 10,000 people. Franklin earned so much money from the slave trade that he eventually owned six plantations and 600 slaves in Louisiana and several thousand acres in Texas—not to mention sizable stock holdings in a Mississippi bank, the Nashville and Gallatin Turnpike Company and a horse track in Nashville. Franklin retired from slave trading in the 1830s to focus on planting. In 1839, he married Adelicia Acklen, a Nashville woman thirty years his junior. She would long outlive him and spend much of his fortune building a Nashville mansion and estate named Belmont.

Despite the size of his enterprise, Isaac Franklin's name appeared only a few times in Tennessee's newspapers during his life. In August 1825—three years before Franklin cofounded Franklin & Armfield—five slaves named Bradley, Shedrick, Bill, Elias and Alfred ran away from his Sumner County plantation. The ad offered $500 for the return of the five—a lot by runaway slave ad standards.

Also, in 1822, 1833 and 1835, Isaac Franklin's name was mentioned in ads published in Tennessee newspapers—each time as the person from whom the enslaved had been acquired. "He [a runaway slave named Isaac Hatchet] was brought to this place by Mr. Isaac Franklin from Virginia, in April last," a Mississippi slaveholder named Joseph Neibert wrote in a runaway slave ad published in the *Nashville Republican* in December 1835.

Franklin died in 1846. Although we will never know how many of his contemporaries looked askance at him for the manner in which he made his fortune, we know wonderful things were written about him when he died. "We knew Isaac Franklin," the *New Orleans Weekly Delta* said after his death. "He was a man of discerning mind, sound judgment, great worth, indomitable spirit and vast enterprise." The Nashville *Republican Banner* had this to say: "He was a high minded, honest man; but what is of more importance; we have reason to believe that he had become a Christian and died in the faith."

MEMPHIS RIVAL VANISHES FROM THE MAP

*W*hen people think of the phrase "ghost town," they normally think of the American West. But Tennessee has a few ghost towns of its own. My favorite—probably the state's most important "ghost town"—was Randolph. It was in Tipton County, about forty miles upstream and on the Mississippi River from Memphis.

In 1818, the U.S. government acquired what is now West Tennessee from the Chickasaw Nation, resulting in the greatest land rush in Tennessee history. Since the Mississippi River was the route taken by people in West Tennessee to get their goods to market, there were immediate movements to build towns along the river. The best-known of these real estate ventures was on the Fourth Chickasaw Bluff, where investors John Overton, James Winchester and Andrew Jackson founded Memphis.

On the Second Chickasaw Bluff, investors started another town in 1823, naming it for Virginia congressman John Randolph. Not only did Randolph have a good landing for Mississippi River flatboats, but it was also only a few miles from where the Hatchie River merged with the Mississippi (a big deal, as the Hatchie is navigable as far inland as Bolivar).

Randolph's heyday was in the 1830s, when it shipped more cotton on the Mississippi River than Memphis. If you had come through Randolph then, you would have found a thousand residents, three warehouses, saloons, schools and four hotels. You would have also found a printing press producing a newspaper called the *Randolph Recorder*.

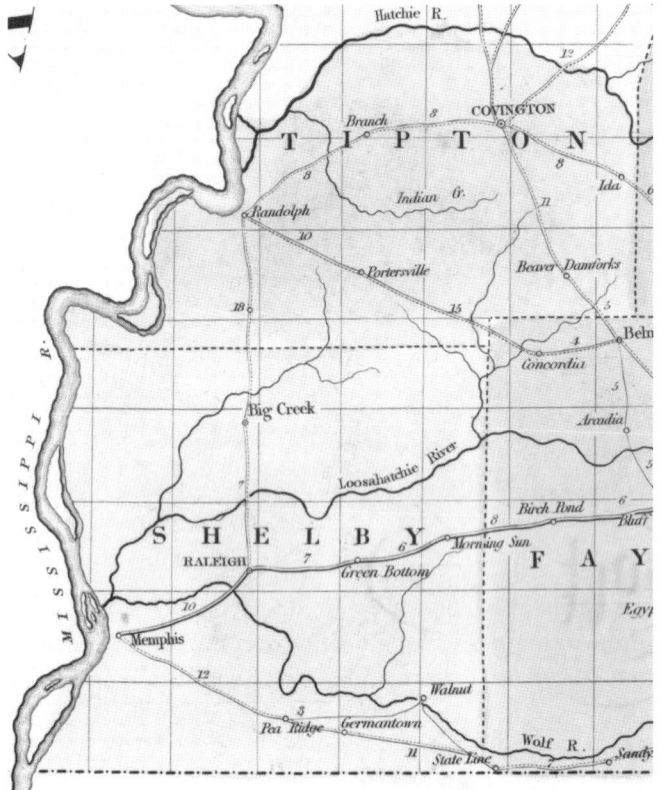

Left: David Burr's 1839 map shows Randolph and Memphis looking comparable in size. *Library of Congress.*

Opposite: The steamboat *Elenora* docked at Randolph in 1912. *Tennessee State Library and Archives.*

The Tennessee State Library and Archives still has back issues of the *Recorder* on microfilm. For several years it came out weekly, although in the summer of 1835 it suspended operations for a time because of a cholera epidemic. According to the *Recorder*, a new steamboat arrived in Randolph just about every day.

Between December 12 and 19, 1834, for example, the *Recorder* reported that eighteen steamboats came through town—ten heading downstream on the Mississippi, seven heading upstream and one floating up the Hatchie. These boats traded everything from cotton and oats to nails and whiskey.

Many people came through Randolph during this era. Some were heading downstream, to New Orleans, or upstream, to St. Louis. Many were heading west to Arkansas, Missouri and Texas. Some people stayed long enough to have been called residents.

Jesse Benton, a colorful character from early Tennessee history who dueled Tennessee governor William Carroll and got in a brawl with Andrew Jackson, lived in Randolph for a time.

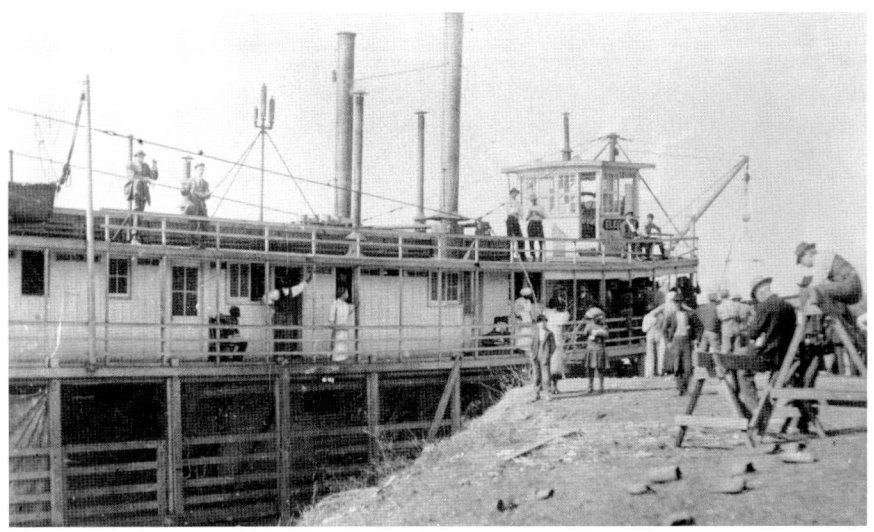

On November 13, 1833, people all over America stared at the sky as one of the largest meteor showers ever took place. Some wondered if the world was coming to an end. Among the people who saw it from Randolph was Congressman David Crockett, who was visiting a friend at the time.

Today, there is nothing on or near the Second Chickasaw Bluff indicating there was a town here in the early nineteenth century. If you come to Randolph today, you can find a small, paved county road, which takes you directly to the river. Thanks to Randolph expert Graydon Swisher, I found a wide path along the river that, he believes, was one of the original thoroughfares of Randolph. But that's about it.

So, why did Memphis thrive and Randolph decline? For one thing, Memphis had more prominent founders, especially Andrew Jackson. I suspect President Jackson may have been the reason the federal government chose Memphis over Randolph for its thrice-per-week mail route, which was huge in that era. In the 1850s, Memphis got the rail connection to Charleston, while Randolph never got a railroad. As the years passed, it also became clear that Memphis has a superior foundation: a "shelf" of sandstone beneath the mud that made for more stable building foundations. Meanwhile, in Randolph, the ground underneath people's feet was literally giving way. In fact, large parts of what were once the town of Randolph have now fallen into the river.

Many of Randolph's buildings were still standing when the Civil War broke out. Early in the conflict, the Confederate government built two forts at Randolph: Fort Randolph and Fort Wright (tearing down many of the

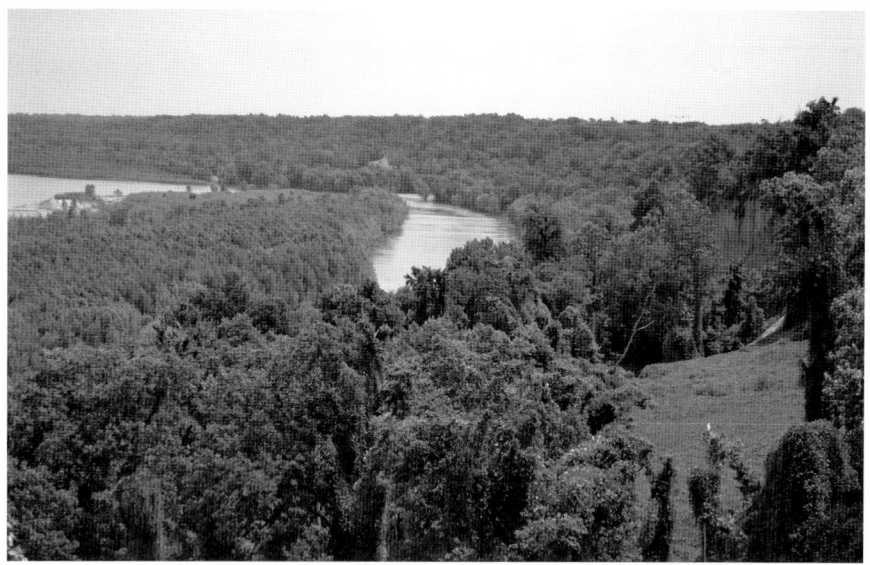

The former site of Randolph. *Author's collection.*

town's abandoned buildings in the process). The Confederate army also operated boot camps here for soldiers throughout Tennessee; it was here that Private Nathan Bedford Forrest began military training.

The Confederate government didn't have much of a navy to help defend its fortifications along the Mississippi. Forts Randolph and Wright were abandoned by Confederate forces in the summer of 1862. A few months later, after Rebel guerrillas were traced to the area, General William T. Sherman, then in charge of the captured city of Memphis, ordered his army to burn what was left of Randolph to the ground. Almost nothing is left of these Civil War fortifications other than an underground magazine where the Confederates stored gunpowder.

Today, most of the land that was Randolph, Fort Randolph and Fort Wright is on private property, so you have to be careful about just showing up and exploring. However, the Tennessee Parks and Greenways Foundation has purchased a nineteen-acre tract where we believe the heart of Randolph to have been, and the Mississippi River Corridor is working on a plan to turn the place into a park and river center.

Who knows? Archaeologists may one day dig up some of the relics left behind at this interesting and unspoiled place on the Mississippi River—at least those that haven't fallen into the river.

DISNEY MOVIES
AND COONSKIN CAPS

*L*ike many people of my generation, I grew up aware of the legend of David Crockett. I saw the Walt Disney movie and the television show. I even had a fake coonskin cap. I have also become long aware of the monuments to Crockett from one end of Tennessee to the other. But I had never read a biography of the man until recently, when I read a new one by Michael Wallis, along with Crockett's autobiography, published two years before he died.

The main thing I wanted to know was "Why is this man so famous?" Here are some things I learned:

Today, people often refer to this man as "Davy" Crockett, but he never signed his name that way. The reason we call him "Davy" is because of a song written in the 1950s, a time when there was a national craze for all things Crockett.

David Crockett is one of the most famous people to ever come from Tennessee. But he was never the president, never the governor and never a general. The highest political rank Crockett achieved was as a member of the U.S. House of Representatives, where he represented West Tennessee.

Crockett was born on August 17, 1786, which means he was born before Tennessee existed. Technically, Crockett was born in the state of Franklin, which we now refer to as the Lost State of Franklin.

Crockett's father, John Crockett, was not a good provider. At one point, John "leased" David to another man to help pay his debts (a practice not uncommon at that time). The closest thing to a father figure for David

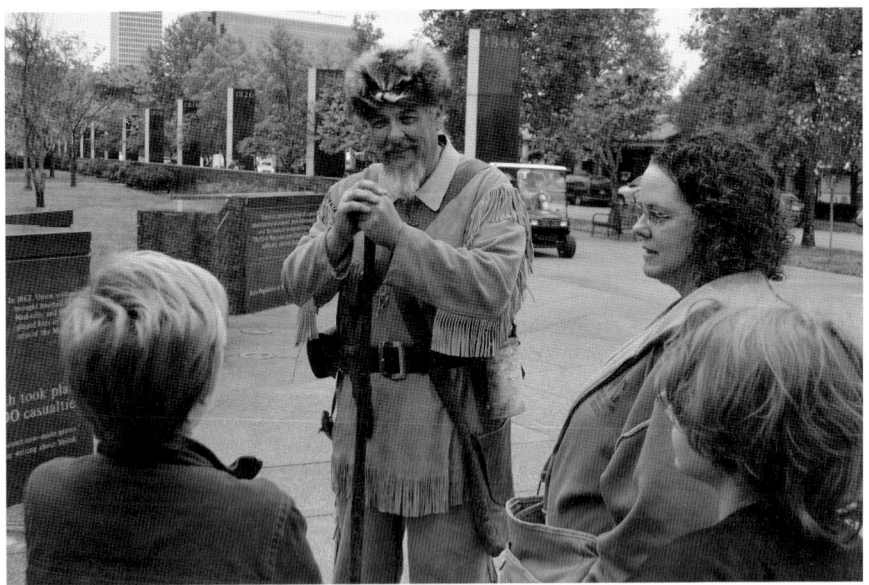

A David Crockett reenactor at the Bicentennial Capitol Mall State Park in Nashville. *Author's collection.*

Crockett appears to have been John Canaday. Canaday, a Quaker, ran a farm in what is now Hamblen County. Crockett worked and lived with him from the time he was sixteen until he was about nineteen. It was under his tutelage that Crockett learned to read and write.

David Crockett was not always successful with the ladies. In his autobiography, he describes two instances where he fell in love, only to end up with a broken heart. One of them was with a girl named Margaret Elder, who married someone else even after Crockett had obtained a marriage license. "My heart was bruised, and my spirits were broken down," he wrote. "So I bid her farewell, and turned my lonesome and miserable steps back again homeward, concluding that I was only born for hardships, misery and disappointment."

Crockett was restless, to say the least. He was born along the Nolichucky River (in present-day Greene County), and his father moved the family to a tavern (in Hamblen County). He spent about three years as a teenager roaming and living alone in various parts of Virginia. As an adult, David Crockett lived in what is now Jefferson, Lincoln, Franklin, Lawrence and Gibson Counties of Tennessee.

Crockett twice volunteered to fight in the Creek Wars. He proved valuable to his comrades as a scout and hunter, and he also saw combat. At one point, he watched about fifty Creek warriors burned to death in a house from where they were fighting. But as fate would have it, Crockett missed both the Battle of Horseshoe Bend and the Battle of New Orleans.

Crockett's political career began in Lawrence County, where he was elected colonel of the local militia and later state representative. Crockett was also part of the local body that chose the site for the Lawrence County Courthouse.

Crockett married twice. His first marriage, to Polly Finley, produced three children. She died shortly after he got back from the Creek Wars and was buried in Franklin County. A few months later, Crockett married Elizabeth Patton. David and Elizabeth had three more children but do not appear to have had a close marriage, as he was always away hunting or in Congress.

After he remarried, Crockett set off on a hunting trip with some friends to what is now Alabama. During the trip, Crockett contracted malaria and couldn't walk because he was so sick. He was rescued by some Choctaw Indians, who took him to a cabin where he was nursed back to health. By the time Crockett made it back to his cabin in Tennessee, his wife believed him to be dead.

Like his father, Crockett was an abject failure as a businessman. One of his schemes was a mill, distillery and gunpowder factory in Lawrence County. That venture failed when Shoal Creek flooded. A few years later, in Gibson County, Crockett went into the timber business. The plan was to chop down hundreds of trees, cut them into staves, float them down the Obion and Mississippi Rivers, and sell them in New Orleans. Unfortunately, the flatboats on which Crockett was delivering his timber harvest capsized in the Mississippi, and he nearly drowned.

When he was originally elected to Congress, Crockett was an ally of Andrew Jackson. But Crockett broke with Jackson and was the only Tennessee congressman who voted against the Indian Removal Act in 1830. From this point onward, Jackson and Crockett were political enemies.

Crockett originally became famous because of stories he would tell other congressmen and reporters about hunting for bears, fighting in the Creek War, floating down the Mississippi, and other adventures. Reporters wrote articles about him and he became one of the best-known personalities in what was then known as the West.

In 1831, a play called *The Lion of the West* became a hit in New York. Its main character, Colonel Nimrod Wildfire, is a storyteller wearing a buckskin shirt and coonskin cap, clearly based on David Crockett. This play made Crockett even more famous and resulted in the publication of

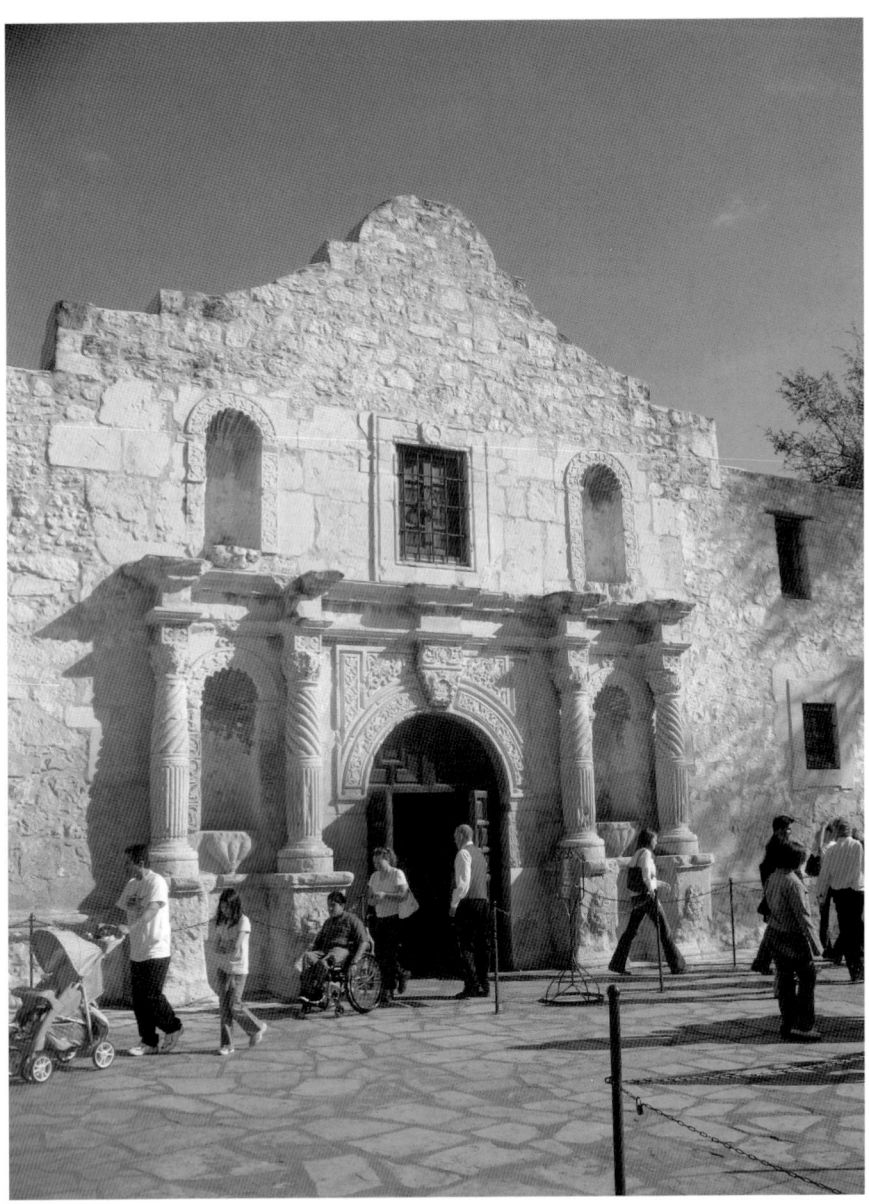

The Alamo in San Antonio, Texas. *Author's collection.*

a biography of him that he didn't write, had nothing to do with and from which he made no money.

Crockett's best friend in Congress was Thomas Chilton of Kentucky, who broke with President Jackson in much the same way Crockett had. Chilton ghost-wrote Crockett's best-selling 1834 autobiography, *A Narrative of the Life of David Crockett of the State of Tennessee*. It is hard to know how accurate this book is, especially since Crockett had a tendency to stretch the truth. (He claims to have killed more than one hundred bears in a seven-month span in West Tennessee, for instance.) But Crockett's humor comes through in his autobiography. He mentions a woman he met who was "well enough to smartness, but she was as ugly as a stone fence." He admits that as the years passed, he was "better at increasing my family than my fortune." And speeches in Congress, Crockett says, were so boring that "it's harder than splitting gum logs in August to stay awake."

So why did Crockett leave Tennessee? In 1834, after a successful book tour, he lost his bid for reelection to Congress. Having heard his friend Sam Houston talk about all the opportunities opening up in Texas, Crockett decided to go there himself. He left by way of Memphis and enjoyed himself on that last night in Tennessee. "Since you have chosen to elect a man with a timber toe to succeed me, you may all go to hell and I will go to Texas," he reportedly said there (in reference to his political opponent's wooden leg).

Why is Crockett so well known, even today? My theory has to do with the manner in which he died and the fame he experienced before his death. There are very few people in American history who were famous *before* they were killed in battle. Crockett was. He was a well-known U.S. congressman, the basis of a popular play and the subject of several books. Then, in January 1836, he went to Texas. He immediately enlisted in the army there and went to the Alamo. We are not certain whether he died fighting or whether he was taken prisoner and executed.

Regardless of his fate, the man who spent almost his entire life in Tennessee belongs to Tennessee.

CROCKETT LOSES HIS PANTS

*H*ere's a story about how David Crockett lost his pants but won an election. It originally came from Crockett's autobiography, and this is an abridged version of it.

In 1825, Crockett lived in a cabin in West Tennessee in what is now Gibson County. His favorite thing to do was hunt, sometimes for a few hours and sometimes for a few days. They didn't have cellphones back then. His wife didn't like it when he wandered off and wasn't heard from for a week. But such was the life of Elizabeth Crockett.

A lot more things were made of wood back then than there are today. Buckets were made of wood. Whiskey was shipped in big wooden barrels. Even the wheels on horse carriages were made of wood. All you had to do was get the wood to a town, where the factories were located. That was the hard part.

David Crockett came up with a plan to make money. He and some other men would chop down trees and cut them up into pieces called staves. They would stack the staves on two huge log rafts and then float the rafts down the Obion River to where it meets the Mississippi River. From there they would float downstream to New Orleans and sell the staves. What a great plan! What could go wrong?

Crockett hired some men to help him chop down trees and cut them into staves and make the log rafts. He couldn't afford to pay them yet, so he promised to pay them later, after he'd sold the staves. He also promised to feed them all the bear meat they could eat while they worked.

While all the men were chopping down trees, Crockett was hunting with his dogs. This was his favorite thing to do, and he was a great hunter. But he had to be careful. You see, there had been a lot of big earthquakes a few years earlier. That's why people called West Tennessee "the land of the shakes." Because of these earthquakes, there were big open cracks in the earth. David Crockett was constantly pulling his dogs out of the cracks, and he had to be careful he didn't fall into one himself and never be heard from again.

Crockett brought in a lot of bear meat, and within a few months, his hired hands had chopped thirty thousand staves. It was around March 1826 when Crockett's two rafts, loaded down with wooden staves, shoved off and headed down the Obion River. The river was high and the current moved quickly. The only thing Crockett and his men had to do was use big sticks and the rudder to keep the rafts in the middle of the river. Things went pretty well at first.

When they hit the big river, now that was a different story. From the moment the two flatboats floated out onto the "mighty Mississip," they felt

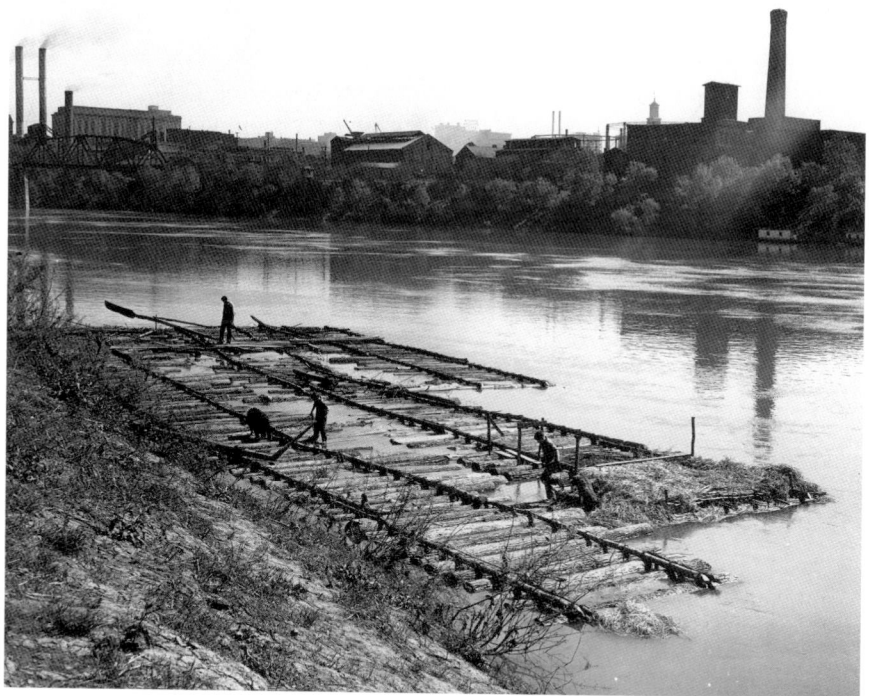

Log rafts were still a frequent sight on the Cumberland River in the early 1900s. *Tennessee State Library and Archives.*

like they were on a fast-moving ocean. They had no idea how to control their rafts, steer their rafts or even stop their rafts. Crockett had his men tie the rafts together. But it didn't help any.

One night, Crockett and his men tried unsuccessfully to steer to the shore. They floated all night, in the dark, huge river, with no idea what was in front of them. At some point, they passed a town. They didn't know what town it was, but they knew it was a town. People waved lanterns, trying to yell instructions on how to stop. "The people would run out with lights, and try to get us to shore, but all in vain," Crockett wrote in his autobiography. But there was no use. They kept on a-going.

Somehow they made it through a turn in the river known as the Devil's Elbow. For a while, Crockett began to think they could make it all the way to New Orleans. But then their luck ran out. The rafts crashed into a large tree stuck in the river. Both boats tipped over, and all the men got thrown overboard. Crockett was lucky he didn't drown.

They all found a pile of driftwood and held on. All the staves were gone, and the men were cold. But they were glad to be alive. "I felt happier and better off than I had in my life before," Crockett wrote, "for I had made such a marvelous escape, that I had forgotten almost else in that; and so I felt prime."

As luck would have it, a boat came by and picked them up. A few hours later, the boat landed in Memphis. It was greeted by a large crowd including Marcus Winchester. He knew who Crockett was and was excited to see him.

Winchester owned a general store in Memphis, not far from the river. This turned out to be a good thing because Crockett was not wearing any pants when the boat fished him out of the Mississippi. Somehow they had fallen off as he struggled to stay alive in the water.

Winchester sent someone to get Crockett a pair of pants. He invited Crockett and his men into his house, which was one of the biggest in Memphis. He fed them and gave them a place to stay. And he loaned Crockett some money.

Crockett sent some of his men home. Then he got on a boat heading downstream in search of what was left of his flatboats. He went all the way to Natchez, Mississippi, but he never found his flatboats or his staves.

It was a long horse ride home. When he got back to Tennessee, Crockett explained the story to all the men he had hired. Since he couldn't pay them, they didn't think the story was funny. Crockett also had to explain it to his wife, Elizabeth, who by this time was used to his tall tales. She wasn't amused either, even when he told her the part about losing his pants.

Other people loved the story though. They lived in other parts of West Tennessee, in counties such as Carroll, Henderson and Madison. When Crockett ran for Congress the next year, he told stories about bear hunting, floating uncontrollably down the Mississippi and being fished out of the Mississippi River with no pants on. People laughed. They elected him to Congress.

And it was there, in Washington, where David Crockett first became a national hero.

TEXTBOOK PHOTO
TO SLAVERY BOOK

*I*t started when John Baker was a seventh grader at Westside Elementary School in Springfield. While paging through his social studies book, the thirteen-year-old was drawn to an 1891 photo showing four elderly people in front of Robertson County's Wessyngton mansion. The people had been enslaved at Wessyngton before the war, the caption said.

Baker's grandmother told him he was related to all four people. "That's my grandmother and grandfather," she told him, pointing to the seated couple. This revelation inspired teenage John Baker to interview older family members (ranging in age from 80 to 107) and family friends. One was Mattie Terry, an elderly lady who lived down the street and who also had family connections to the Wessyngton Plantation.

Terry told Baker stories that her great-grandmother Sarah (an enslaved person at Wessyngton) had told her years before. These included stories about what the slaves did, how hard they worked and even how they got in trouble for praying. "Grandma Sarah told us that prayer meetings had to be held in secret on the plantation," she said. "Slaves put overturned kettles and pots at their doors to muffle the sound of praying and singing."

The more Baker learned, the more he wanted to know. His interest was fueled by the fact that the mansion was still standing and had a documented history. Consisting of more than thirteen thousand acres, Wessyngton had been the largest tobacco plantation in the United States before the Civil War. At that time, its owner, George A. Washington (thought to be a distant relative of the president), had 274 slaves.

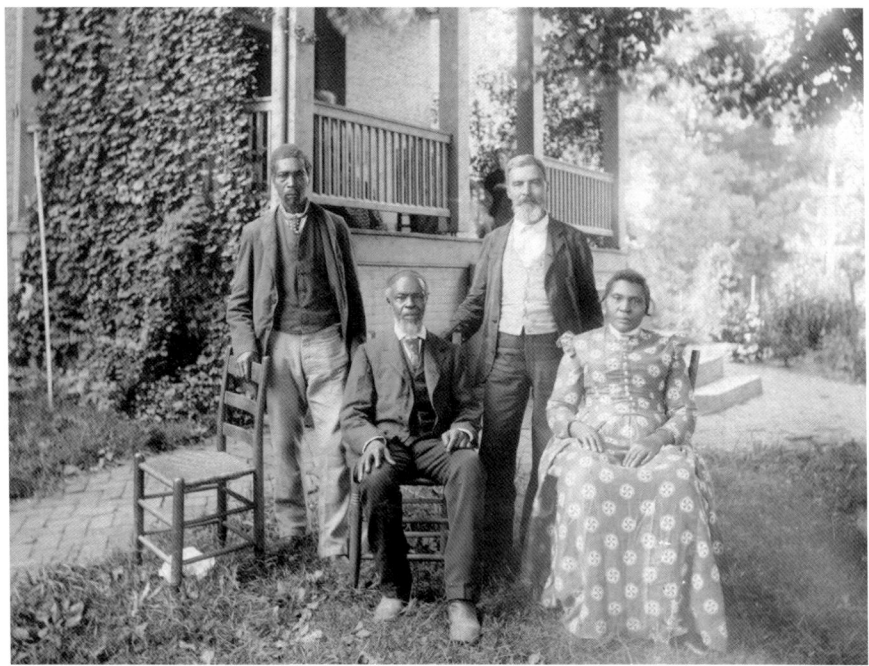

The photo that changed John Baker's life, showing Emmanuel, Henry, Allen and Granville Washington at the Wessyngton Plantation in Robertson County. *Tennessee State Library and Archives.*

Baker took a tour of the Wessyngton Plantation and its grounds, which included former slave cabins. He also visited the Tennessee State Library and Archives and studied its collection of Wessyngton papers, which included letters, newspaper articles, journals, diaries, slave bills of sale and doctor's bills.

In 2009, Simon & Schuster published Baker's book, *The Washingtons of Wessyngton Plantation: Stories of My Family's Journey to Freedom*. It reveals a lot about what slavery was like and how the institution spread throughout Tennessee. For instance, when Wessyngton founder Joseph Washington migrated west from Virginia in 1796, he had only two enslaved people. That number ballooned over the years. One of his first purchases was in 1802, when he acquired two girls named Sarah and Jenny. The bill of sale for Sarah and Jenny is still on file at the Tennessee State Library and Archives.

The slaves at Wessyngton worked in the house and on the grounds. They did most of the construction of the main mansion, including making the bricks from clay. They smoked hams and distilled whiskey (both of which the plantation became famous for). But mostly, they did the planting, caring and harvesting of tobacco.

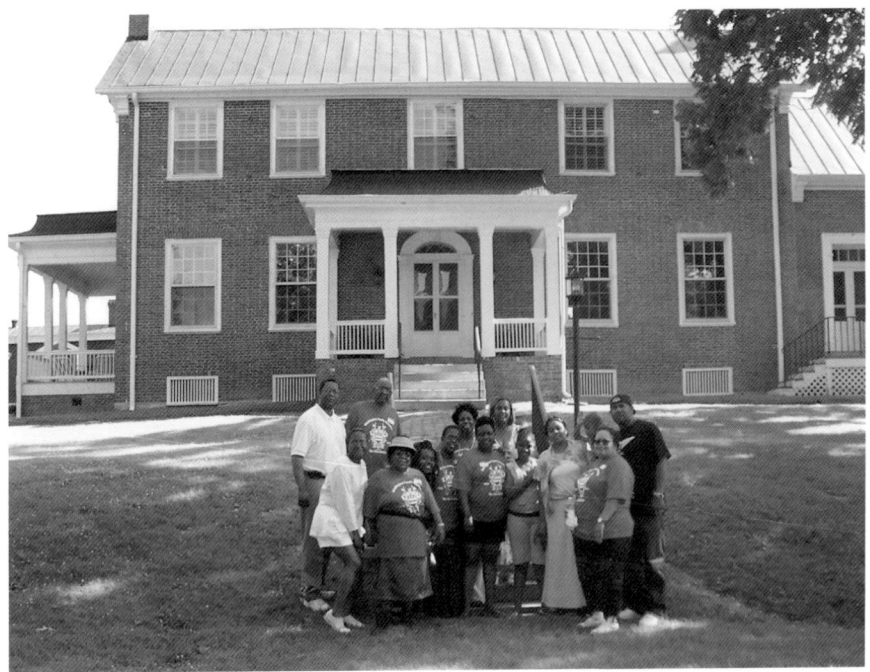

One of the many family reunions that have taken place at the Wessyngton Plantation since John Baker wrote his book. *John Baker.*

Baker documented eighty-eight instances over the years of "slave rebellion"—quarrelling, theft, disturbances, refusal to work and runaways. He found eleven times between 1838 and 1860 when enslaved people tried to escape. The only two of those eleven who made it to free territory were recaptured in Indiana and sent back to Tennessee.

Baker found no record of the Washingtons ever granting freedom to any of their enslaved people. For them, emancipation came during and after the Civil War. At that time, many of the former slaves left the area. But according to Baker's research, nearly one hundred of the former enslaved people remained in Robertson County to work as sharecroppers.

In the process of his research, Baker learned the names, birth and death dates of 445 people who were enslaved at Wessyngton. About 200 of them are buried at Wessyngton, most without marked graves. Descendants of the Washingtons donated funds to erect a monument at the cemetery with all the names of all the people who were enslaved there, known to be buried there or assumed to be buried there. It is a remarkable tribute to the work by John Baker, which began from a photograph in a social studies textbook.

LAND PIRATE'S THUMB

*I*t's the strangest item in the Tennessee Historical Society's collection of which I'm aware. The Tennessee Museum puts it on display once a year. When it does so, there is often an article about it in the Nashville media, along with a photo of it and the little case in which it is stored. It's a human thumb. And it is not just any thumb, mind you. The thumb put on display used to belong to none other than John Murrell.

Who was John Murrell, you ask? An ill-fated hitchhiker? Not exactly. John Murrell was an outlaw who operated in the 1820s and 1830s on the road that most history books refer to as the Natchez Trace, as well as points as far west as Arkansas. It is safe to say that few living Americans have heard of John Murrell. But that has not always been the case.

There have been many books about Murrell. The first was written in the 1830s by Virgil Stewart, who claimed to have spied on Murrell and learned firsthand about Murrell's murders, robberies and his secret crime organization, the "Mystic Clan." Over the years, there have been about a half dozen more. They generally repeat much of the information in Stewart's book, painting a picture of Murrell as a clever, cutthroat, ruthless criminal—a "land pirate," so to speak.

According to most of these books, Murrell routinely latched on to fellow travelers along the Natchez Trace, often in the guise of a friendly traveling preacher. Then, while they were sleeping, he would cut their throats and take their money. Murrell would also preach in town squares while his accomplices picked pockets and stole horses. Murrell also allegedly helped

STEWART'S NARRATIVE.

THE HISTORY OF VIRGIL A. STEWART, and his adventure in capturing and exposing the great WESTERN LAND PIRATE, John A. Murrell and his gang, in connection with the evidence—Also, of the Trials, Confessions and Execution of a number of Murrell's associates in the State of Mississippi in the Summer of 1835, and the execution of five Professional Gamblers by the citizens of Vicksburg, compiled by H. R. HOWARD, 1 vol. duodecimo.

Just published by Harper and Brothers, N. York, and for sale by WHITE & NORVELL, Price $1 50. Nashville.

☞A liberal discount on the above work to WHOLESALE purchasers.

Nov. 14.—1t.

Virgil Stewart's book, in which he alleged to have captured Murrell and his "Mystic Clan," was quite the bestseller in 1830s Tennessee. *From the* National Banner and Nashville Whig, *November 11, 1836.*

slaves escape from bondage, only to trick them and sell them to slave traders. Many books also claim that Murrell planned to incite and profit from a mass slave rebellion, which was to have taken place on Christmas Day 1835. However, the plan was thwarted when Murrell was arrested and convicted for stealing slaves.

Mark Twain talks about John Murrell in his book *Life on the Mississippi*. In *Tom Sawyer*, Tom, Huck and Injun Joe are all searching for Murrell's lost treasure, said to be hidden in a cave near the Mississippi River.

In 1940, Humphrey Bogart played John Murrell in a movie called *Virginia City*. A fictionalized John Murrell appeared in 1950s TV shows such as *The Adventures of Jim Bowie* and *Riverboat*. Murrell was the central figure in the 1960 movie *Natchez Trace* (posters for which hang at the Zaxby's restaurant near the northern terminus of the Natchez Trace Parkway).

All this might make you wonder why our awareness of John Murrell has faded over the years. I have two theories for this. One is that our awareness of just about everything historic and Tennessee has dimmed over the years. But the other reason is that the stories about John Murrell were almost certainly exaggerated during the 120 years after his death, for reasons which should bother us today.

As best I can tell, John Murrell was twice convicted of crimes. The first was in the 1820s in Nashville, when he was branded, whipped and sent to jail for horse theft. The second time was in 1834 in Jackson, when he was convicted of stealing slaves. Murrell was pardoned from prison in 1844 and moved to Pikeville, in Bledsoe County. He died only a few months later. In a deathbed confession, Murrell admitted to many of the crimes he had been charged with. But he said he never killed anyone.

Assuming Murrell was telling the truth, or even if he wasn't telling the complete truth, why did this criminal from Tennessee become so famous? The story may have something to do with the nature of the times.

In the early 1830s, because of the Nat Turner Rebellion in Virginia, white southerners were nervous about the idea of a slave uprising. Virgil Stewart's 1835 written claim that John Murrell and his gang of outlaws were masterminding a slave rebellion was taken seriously at the time. In fact, after the release of Stewart's booklet, many enslaved people throughout the South were questioned and lynched for their alleged roles in the conspiracy, especially in Mississippi.

In modern times, we are familiar with the "Underground Railroad," and we look back with admiration at people who tried to help slaves escape. But in the early 1800s, helping them escape was called "negro stealing." It was a serious crime, punishable by somewhere between two years in the state penitentiary and death by hanging (depending on the decade and the state). Slaveholders and the newspapers supporting them were not averse to spreading stories meant to make enslaved people think twice about running away—especially with the aid of someone they didn't know very well. The John Murrell myth worked to maintain the status quo.

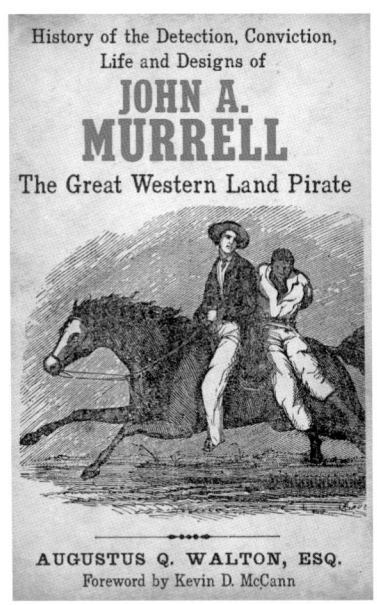

One of the many books about John Murrell.

Finally, here's one more point about the era of John Murrell and his alleged "slave rebellion." The 1830s was the decade in which books about David Crockett were bestsellers. All of these books combined truth with fiction, actual events with ridiculous exaggerations. Even Crockett's own autobiography is filled with tall tales about falling into huge holes and hand-to-hand fighting with black bears. So it is very possible that a story about a simple outlaw could get blown out of proportion.

All of this brings us to the thumb. Sometime after Murrell was buried in 1844, grave robbers allegedly dug up his body at the Smyrna Cemetery near Pikeville. The outlaw's body somehow ended up at a Nashville medical school six decades later. A physician severed one of Murrell's thumbs and donated it to the Tennessee Historical Society in 1895.

This story may be just as preposterous as the one about Murrell's "Mystic Clan" and his planned slave rebellion. It is true that nineteenth-century grave robbers routinely dug up corpses and sold them to medical students as cadavers. But why would grave robbers unearth a corpse in Pikeville and transport it all the way across the state, when there were thousands or more conveniently located cemeteries?

The more likely scenario is that medical students gave names to all their cadavers (as medical students probably still do). Since they all knew the legend about Murrell, they gave that name to one of them and it stuck. Eventually, someone sliced off his thumb and donated to the Tennessee Historical Society as a bit of a joke.

"How this mummy came into the Medical Department of the University of Nashville, and where it rested from 1838 to 1851 or whether the whole thing is a fanciful romance, a hoax out of whole cloth I am trying to determine," wrote Dr. S.S. Crockett of the Tennessee Historical Society in 1917. "The more I look into the matter, the more I believe that the tradition was probably without any foundations whatever."

As for me, the more I read about John Murrell, his "Mystic Clan" and his thumb, the more I come to the same conclusion about these stories. But I'm sure that won't stop people from making movies and writing ghost stories. And it won't stop people from being interested in the mysterious thumb and its cute coffin put on display every year at the Tennessee State Museum.

RED CLAY'S SOMBER STORY

*R*ed Clay is a state historic park about an hour's drive from Chattanooga in Bradley County. This is its story.

The Cherokee Nation once ruled over a large part of the southeast United States. But as white settlers moved west and forced their way onto Cherokee land, Cherokee leaders signed away or sold large chunks of the land, sometimes under political or military pressure. By the 1820s, Cherokee controlled only part of what is now southeast Tennessee, southwest North Carolina, northeast Alabama and northwest Georgia.

In spite of the loss of so much of their land, most Cherokees assumed they would be allowed to stay in this part of the country forever. After all, they had coexisted peacefully with the U.S. government for more than a generation—ever since the Nickajack Expedition of 1794, when white settlers defeated the warlike Chickamaugan band of the Cherokee Nation.

Many Cherokees had fought for the U.S. government, such as at the Battle of Horseshoe Bend against the Creeks. More importantly, the Cherokee Nation had largely adopted white ways—becoming farmers, taking on a democratic form of government under a constitution, adopting Christianity and even creating a written language. By the 1820s, Cherokees were more likely to be literate in the Cherokee language than white settlers in this part of the country were to be literate in the English language. They even had a written newspaper, the *Cherokee Phoenix*.

In 1828, however, two things occurred that sealed the fate of the Cherokee Nation east of the Mississippi River. First, gold was discovered on Cherokee

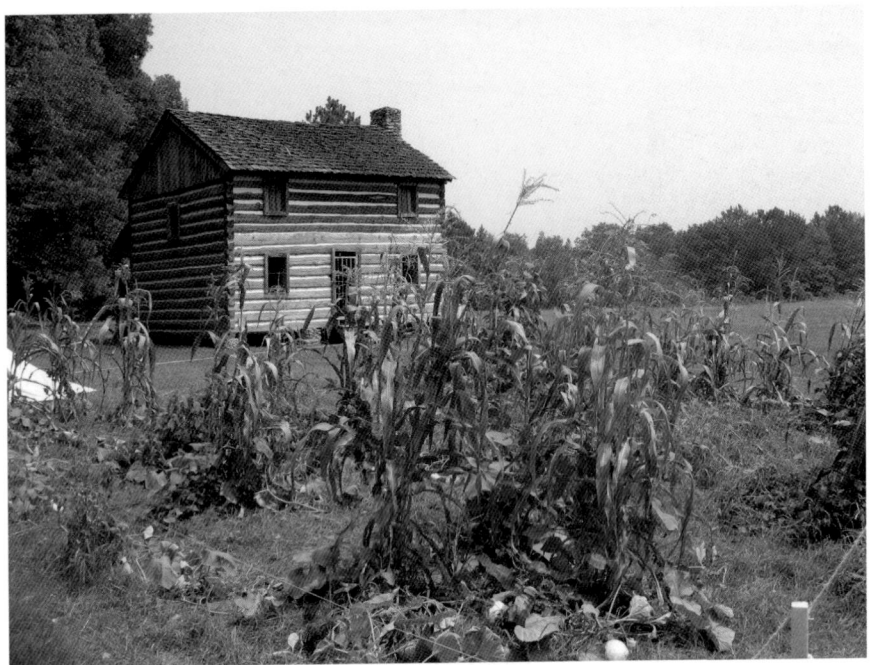

This cabin and farm at Red Clay State Historic Park illustrates the point that before the Trail of Tears, the Cherokee Indian Nation had largely adopted American ways. *Author's collection.*

land in Georgia, resulting in a massive encroachment by white settlers onto Cherokee property. Then Andrew Jackson was elected president. Although he could be kind to individual Native Americans, Jackson did not believe Native American culture could coexist with the United States. He pursued a policy of removal—of forcing the Cherokees off their land and relocating them to points west of the Mississippi River.

By 1832, the Georgia legislature had taken away all Cherokee legal rights, taken the Cherokees' land and made it a crime for Cherokees to hold political meetings. At that point, the Cherokee Nation moved its capital to a site just north of the Tennessee/Georgia state line (Red Clay). There was a spring on the site called Blue Hole Spring that is still there today. There were no structures there, so the Cherokees built a few cabins and a council house.

A council was a time when the Cherokee people came together to meet and for their leaders to discuss things important to the nation. Councils generally lasted between two weeks and a month. The Cherokees had eleven separate councils at Red Clay between 1832 and 1838.

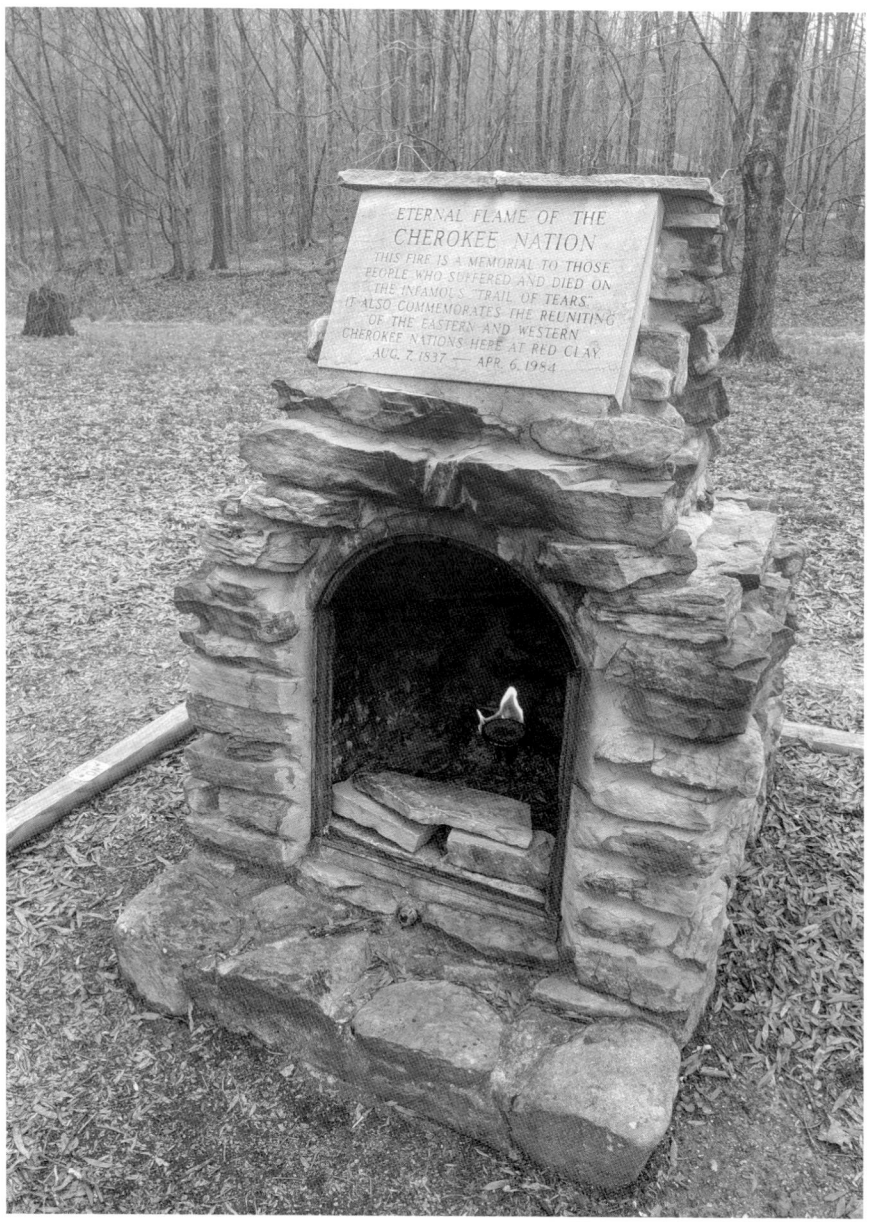

The eternal flame at Red Clay State Historic Park. *Author's collection.*

According to first-person accounts, there was still some festivity at the Red Clay councils. Children played and adults apparently spent most of their time holding Baptist church services. But these were desperate times for the Cherokees. In spite of President Jackson's insistence that they would have to leave, the Cherokee people still held out hope that John Ross, their principal chief, would be able to work out a deal under which they could stay. The Cherokee people had a good legal case, since the U.S. Supreme Court under John Marshall had ruled that the 1830 Indian Removal Act was unconstitutional.

At Red Clay, the Cherokees realized the U.S. Supreme Court ruling would not help them. Here they also learned that a small group of Cherokee leaders (led by Major Ridge) had signed the Treaty of New Echota, which purportedly sold all the Cherokee land east of the Mississippi River to the U.S. government.

When John Ross learned about this treaty, he tried hard to get the Senate to reject it (an effort that failed by one vote). To that effort, more than fifteen thousand Cherokees (practically the entire nation) signed a petition protesting the treaty and disavowing those who had signed it. But the U.S. government used this treaty as final justification to force the Cherokees off their land.

In the fall of 1838, the U.S. Army began forcing Indians into staging camps near the Tennessee River. From there, some went downriver on boats, while others marched northwest, toward their eventual destination (present-day Oklahoma).

Today, we estimate that four thousand of the fifteen thousand Cherokees died either along the way or in the holding camps, which is why it is referred to as the Trail of Tears. The trip was especially hard on the elderly and young children. Those who died were usually buried in unmarked graves, which are now all over Tennessee and Arkansas.

After the Cherokees left, all the structures at Red Clay were torn down and the land became part of a privately owned farm. It remained so until 1979, when its many owners sold the land to the State of Tennessee to be used as a historic park. Among the structures you will find there today are a visitors' center and replicas of the council house, a small Cherokee farm and the small cabins that might have been there during Red Clay's short stint as Cherokee capital.

BAREFOOTED AND BADLY CLAD

*H*istorical fiction has its place. But widely read and watched historical fiction—*War and Peace*, *Gone with the Wind*, *Inherit the Wind* and so on—can trick people into thinking that a quote or story made up by a writer is true when it isn't.

Over the years, I've found this to be the case regarding the Trail of Tears. In fact, the education director at the Museum of the Cherokee Indian in North Carolina once told me that some of the first-person accounts of the Trail of Tears she had encountered had, upon further review, come from historical fiction. I therefore resolved to round up many of the stories published in newspapers when the event took place.

In this section, I will allow these primary sources to speak for themselves. But I need to explain a few things in advance: The phrase "Trail of Tears" was not used in the 1830s. The forced migration of native peoples to locations west of the Mississippi River was broadly known as "Indian Removal" and in Tennessee as the "Cherokee Emigration." The Treaty of New Echota—the agreement used by the U.S. government to justify the removal of the Cherokee Nation—was then referred to as the "Treaty of 1835."

In late 1837, a delegation of Cherokee chiefs led by John Ross went to Washington to negotiate with the U.S. government and to communicate the fact that many members of the Cherokee Nation were opposed to the Treaty of New Echota.

Fort Cass was a U.S. Army fort located in what is now Charleston, Tennessee (in Bradley County).

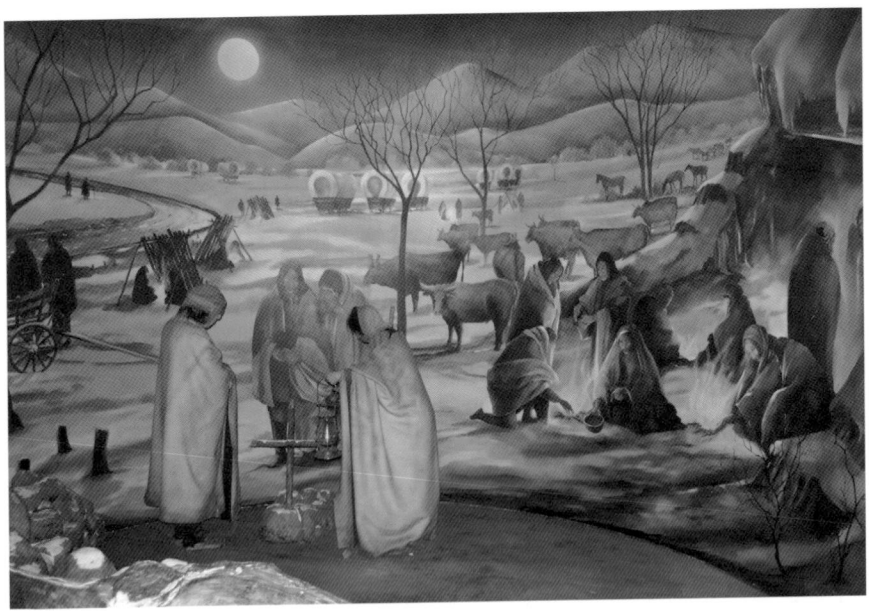

A diorama at the Cherokee Indian Museum in Cherokee, North Carolina, that illustrates the Trail of Tears. *Author's collection.*

The series of events that would eventually lead to the creation of the Cherokee Indian Reservation in North Carolina started on November 1, 1838, when several extended family members of a Cherokee chief named Tsali fought back, killing two U.S. Army soldiers.

Following are quotes from some of the articles I found in newspapers of that era, most of them in Tennessee.

Athens Journal, December 22, 1836: "We have no great objection to the treaty [of 1835]. But we have before said, and we now send it as part of our talk on this occasion, that the treaty was made without the assent or approbation of either the Cherokee nation or their delegated agents."

Nashville Republican, May 5, 1837: "We are rejoiced that the Cherokees have, at length, been influenced to pursue the only course which, in our opinion, can save them from that annihilation, as a nation, which has always befallen every Indian stage, surrounded by the white people."

Baltimore American, January 25, 1838: "The president [Martin Van Buren] regards the treaty of 1835 as the law of the land, that no negotiation therefore can be opened on the basis proposed, and that the Cherokees are expected to remove at the period stipulated by that treaty. It also censures the Delegation for holding out false hopes to the people."

Nashville Union, April 21, 1838: "One of the enrolling agents has visited eleven of the Cherokee towns, containing about two thousand inhabitants, and that at least three fourths of them refused to emigrate. They said that Ross had told them to go home and go work, and that they would not remove until ordered by him. The determination of this deluded race to remain in their present country has excited the alarm of the authorities of Georgia."

Nashville Union, May 23, 1838, quoting General Winfield Scott: "Cherokees! The President of the United States has sent me with a powerful army, to cause you, in obedience to the Treaty of 1835, to join that part of your people who have already established in prosperity, on the other side of the Mississippi."

Athens Journal, June 8, 1838: "The troops in the Cherokee country are making rapid progress in collecting the Indians. Some thousands have already been assembled. They make no resistance whatsoever but quietly and quickly pack up their household affairs, and proceed without any forcible constraint to the place prepared for their reception."

Knoxville Register, July 18, 1838: "We learn from Captain James Morrow that nearly all of the Cherokees, to the number of thirteen or fourteen thousand, have been collected by General Scott and are stationed at the Agency, Chattanooga, and a point between Red Clay and Cleveland, where they will be kept until 1st September, unless before that time they may wish to be taken to their new country west of the Mississippi."

(Detroit) *Democratic Free Press*, July 18, 1838: "As the Indians had not prepared themselves for the removal, it must be attended with great suffering and privation, and also with the total loss of the little personal property which they may be possessed, and which they can neither sell nor carry with them. They are, it appears, 'collected' and marched off in crowds without an opportunity to make any arrangements for a comfortable journey."

Nashville Union, August 15, 1838: "The conference between Gen. Scott and the Cherokee council is at length ended. The Chiefs of the Nation have undertaken the transportation of the remainder of the people to their new homes. It is now a National movement on the part of the Indians, and for the first time there is something like a unanimity of feeling and concurrence of the whole tribe....It is computed that all the Indians can be removed in twelve detachments and that the last will leave by the 20th of October."

Republican Banner, August 29, 1838: "The *Hamilton Gazette* states that serious dissensions exist between the Ross and Bell parties, which it is feared will obstruct the consummation of the contract between the government and the council for removal of the Cherokees. A number of prominent men, it is said, positively avow that they will not submit to emigrate under the auspices of Ross and in the manner appointed."

(Macon) *Weekly Telegraph*, September 18, 1838: "Will be sold on the first Tuesday in October next, before the courthouse...lot of land number 116, 11th district, 3d section, originally Cherokee now Murray County."

Hamilton Gazette, October 1, 1838: "It is estimated that it will take each detachment eighty or a hundred days to perform the trip. This will throw them in the cold States, through which they must pass, in mid-winter. Their sufferings will be great. Half-clad—barefoot and bare-headed, as most of them will be, they will be almost cut off, by the action of the keen winds, whistling through their thin garments, and cold snows falling upon their unprotected heads. The stout and athletic middle-aged man may withstand it with comparatively little oppression; but the aged, and little children, will fall before the pitiless peltings of the storm, like the leaves of autumn beneath the influence of the white frost."

Newbern (NC) Spectator, September 28, 1838: "The Cherokees are a solemn and orderly people. On Sunday last I was still at Fort Cass. At the surrounding camps religious exercises were strictly observed. The gospel was proclaimed by full-blooded Cherokees in their native language—the holy sacrament administered, and three were baptized. Everything was conducted in a manner so earnest and solemn as to cause the white man to blush. The preachers referred to the present condition of their people, exhorting them to use no violence against their oppressors; but to submit all things to an overruling Providence."

Republican Banner, October 9, 1838: "The Hairs, Bushyheads, Hixes and Banjes detachments, consisting of one thousand each, are on the road to

THE CHEROKEES.

The second detachment of the emigrating Cherokees passed through Nashville Monday on their way to the 'Far West.' They lay encamped near Foster's mill on the Murfreesboro' Turnpike for several days, and while there were visited by many of our citizens. We had no opportunity of seeing this miserable remnant of a warlike race, in camp; but a worthy subscriber residing in the country, writes that he was present several times, and regrets to say that many of the Indians appeared extremely needy in apparel. Barefooted and badly clad, they cannot all hope to withstand the fatigues of travel and the inclemency of the season. Disease and perhaps death must be the portion of scores of their number before they reach the Western frontier. Indeed four or five were buried near town, and not less than 50 were on the sick list when they passed through on Monday. The same correspondent asks us to propose to our fellow citizens some means of relief for the detachments yet to pass, but we confess our inability to do so, beyond suggesting the propriety and humanity of contributing such donations of clothing &c. as might be conveniently spared and would prove of real service to the recipients. In this way the ladies—always first in works of charity, could do much to alleviate the sufferings of our red brethren.

We understand that a minister of the gospel accompanies each detachment, through whom all donations of clothing could be judiciously distributed.

A public meeting is alluded to; but this we deem rather impracticable. It would be a serious if not difficult task to afford permanent relief, to so large a body of emigrants on a notice of three or four days. The time is too short and the objects of charity nearer home, too numerous, to bear us out in such an undertaking.

Could Gen. Scott—whose humane and judicious policy in the Cherokee removal, we have frequently had cause to advert to, have foreseen the extraordinary drought of the season, he would doubtless have ordered the removal to commence at an earlier day than the one determined upon. By starting the emigrants before the mountain streams dried up, the emigating parties would have avoided the inconveniences of a want of water as well as the 'early blasts of October and November. A suggestion to this purport was respectfully made to the General in a letter from Governor Cannon in June last, but as he had not then completed his arrangements (and it was the earnest wish of the nation to remain until September,) a different course was concluded upon. The first of September found the country parched up by an unprecedented drought—the emigration could not safely commence, and the unhappy consequence is, that the middle of December will scarcely find the poor Indian seated at his new fireside in the West.

Nashville Whig, October 24, 1838.

their new homes....We are informed that the health and condition of the Indians is much improved from the circumstance of the whooping cough and measles having passed through them."

(Lexington) *Kentucky Gazette*, October 11, 1838: "Two parties of 1,000 or 1,200 each, started by land, under the Ross contract, but were compelled to halt at Blythe's ferry, TN, for rain, the drought being so great as to endanger the safety of the emigrants."

Republican Banner, October 16, 1838: "As our paper was going to press, a detachment of a thousand or twelve hundred Cherokees passed through our city on their way to the west. We understand that another and larger detachment will pass this place tomorrow or next day."

Nashville Whig, October 24, 1838: "The second detachment of the emigrating Cherokees passed through Nashville Monday on their way to the 'Far West.' They lay encamped near Foster's mill on the Murfreesboro Turnpike for several days, and while there were visited by many of our citizens....A worthy subscriber residing in the country writes that he was present several times, and regrets to say that many of the Indians appeared extremely needed in apparel. Barefooted and badly clad, they cannot all hope to withstand the fatigues of travel and the inclemency of the season. Disease and perhaps death must be the portion of scores of their number before they reach the Western frontier. Indeed four or five were buried near town, and not less than 50 were on the sick list when they passed through on Monday."

Georgia Pioneer, October 30, 1838: "Two detachments of Cherokees left the week previous for their homes in the far west, leaving but three or four detachments, which will take up the line of march in the course of a week or two. The sick and the aged, the blind and the lame, will remain until the rising of the waters, they being unable to go by land."

Republican Banner, November 5, 1838: "Another detachment of Cherokee Indians passed through this place on yesterday."

Natchez Weekly Courier, November 23, 1838: "The emigration of these Indians had been attended to with no serious difficulty until the evening of the 1st. While three U.S. soldiers were escorting a small party near the Little Tennessee River, they suddenly attacked the soldiers, killed two of them and made their escape to the mountains. The 4th Regiment of Infantry has been ordered to pursue and capture these marauders. The number of Cherokees remaining is very small, fifteen thousand of them having been sent out of the country since the 1st June....The work of emigration will be very soon completed and the Red Man will have to bid adieu to the homes of the fathers within the limits of the Carolinas and Georgia. They have turned their faces towards the setting sun—emblematic of the utter extinction that awaits their race."

Fayetteville Weekly, November 28, 1838: "Gen. Scott reports to the War Department that there about 200 of the tribe, including 40 warriors, who have concealed themselves in the mountains of this state, eluding all efforts to capture them and disregarding all persuasions to emigrate. He had dispatched a strong force to ferret them out."

Nashville Republican, December 1, 1838: "The last detachment of the emigrating Cherokees, numbering 1,700 or 1,800 persons, is now at Mill Creek, about four miles west of this city. Winter is approaching so rapidly that some of the detachments will be compelled to halt far short of their ultimate destination. A point upon the Ohio, convenient to navigation, will probably be selected for their winter quarters. When navigation becomes good in the spring, they can easily be transported by water to their future homes."

Tennessee Baptist, December 1, 1838: "Four detachments of the emigrating Cherokees have, within a few days, passed through our city, and seven others are behind and expecting to pass in a week or two. They average about a thousand each....During two of three days that their business detained them in the vicinity of this city we had the pleasure of some intercourse with these and others of our Cherokee brethren; and more lovely and excellent Christians we have never seen."

Republican Banner, December 11, 1838, quoting President Martin Van Buren: "It affords me sincere pleasure to apprize you of the entire removal of the Cherokee nation of Indians to their new homes west of the Mississippi."

ENGINEER PUTS CHATTANOOGA ON MAP

*W*hen it comes to history, politicians and generals get all the glory, while no one gives credit to the engineers. Stephen Harriman Long is an interesting example. Were it not for Long, the city of Chattanooga might not exist.

The state of Georgia was about ten years ahead of Tennessee when it came to railroads. By the mid-1830s, the Peach State had several railroads in the works with names such as the Central of Georgia Railway and the Georgia Railroad. All were intended to link the Atlantic coastline and Savannah River with points in the interior of the state.

Then, in 1836, the Georgia government took the rather unusual step of starting a taxpayer-owned railroad called the Western and Atlantic. The idea of the W&A was to connect the interior of the state—the intended destination of the many railroads already in the works—to the Tennessee River. The W&A hired Stephen Harriman Long, an explorer and cartographer who had helped build the Baltimore and Ohio Railroad, to be its lead surveyor.

Sometime in the late 1830s, a member of Long's team drove a stake in the ground seven miles east of the Chattahoochee River. The town that grew up around "Zero Mile Post" was originally called Terminus.

Long and his colleagues then surveyed what route best connected Terminus to the Tennessee River. There were two main choices. One was for the railroad to head west to Gunter's Landing—the place in northeast Alabama where the Tennessee River abruptly turns west. The other was for

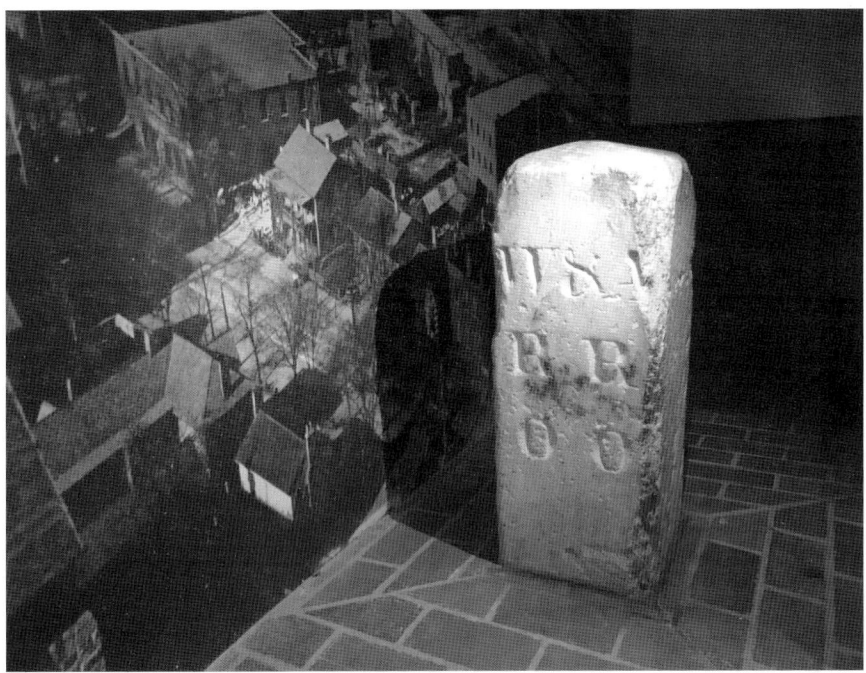

"Zero Mile Post," the marker that used to sit where the Western and Atlantic Railroad terminated in Atlanta. *Jim Hodgson/Wikimedia Commons.*

the railroad to head northwest to Ross's Landing—another place where the river turns west (but this time in southeast Tennessee).

Meanwhile, navigation problems along the Tennessee River were foremost on everyone's mind. The Tennessee River passed through many barriers to navigation just downstream from Chattanooga—boulders, shoals, whirlpools and other obstacles with names such as the Whirl, the Suck and the Boiling Pot. These river barriers would be eliminated when the Tennessee Electric Power Company built Hales Bar Dam three quarters of a century later. However, in the 1830s, they were still huge impediments to commerce.

Long and his team studied both routes and recommended Ross's Landing. Their report was published in the September 18, 1839 Nashville *Republican Banner.* Long pointed out the following:

- The Gunter's Landing route would be about forty-five miles longer than the Ross's Landing route.
- The Gunter's Landing route would have to pass over Alabama's Sand Mountain, "which can only be crossed by

means of three, perhaps four, inclined planes, at an ascent of more than 100 feet per mile." And "there is no gap or depression in Sand Mountain by which these appalling difficulties can be avoided."

- Gunter's Landing was more inclined to flood than Ross's Landing.

The other reason many officials favored the Ross's Landing over the Gunter's Landing is a belief that either the State of Tennessee or a private company would build another railroad heading southeast from Nashville to hook up with it. A route directly west from central Georgia to Gunter's Landing wouldn't exactly be taking the short route toward Nashville—not to mention Louisville, Kentucky, farther north.

The railroad went along with Stephen Long's recommendations. To summarize a lot of history, the town that sprung up at the former site of Ross's Landing became known as Chattanooga. Gunter's Landing changed its name to Guntersville. Terminus changed its name to Marthasville. Then, so the story goes, another railroad engineer named John Edgar Thompson came up with the idea that the place instead be called "Atlantica-Pacifica." By 1845, that had been shortened to Atlanta.

About the same time Marthasville changed its name to Atlanta, construction began on the Western and Atlantic Railroad. The W&A made it to Cartersville by the end of 1846 and Dalton by the end of 1847. The last fifty miles of the railroad took much longer than the first hundred miles because a 1,500-foot tunnel had to be dug just north of Dalton, in the town now known as Tunnel Hill.

The ceremony marking the completion of the Western and Atlantic Railroad occurred on December 1, 1849—the day the first locomotive arrived in Chattanooga from Atlanta. A railroad official dipped a cup into the Tennessee River, mixed it with salt water he had brought from Savannah and then poured them both into the river. According to the *Atlanta Constitution*, "He pronounced that this mingling of the waters of the three states symbolized their union

CHATTANOOGA VICTORIOUS.

Our fine-spirited friend of the Hamilton Gazette is in perfect raptures. He has received from one of the Commissioners the "glorious news" that the north-western terminus of the Western and Atlantic Railroad has been located to terminate at Chattanooga. The location was made by the unanimous vote and consent of the Commissioners. Brother of the Gazette! we join you in three hearty cheers for Chattanooga!

Nashville *Republican Banner*, February 26, 1838.

and fraternity which must be as lasting as their waterways"—a concept to be tested sooner, and more seriously, than anyone present could have imagined.

Stephen Harriman Long was not present that day. As superintendent of the construction of the Marine Hospital in Louisville, Kentucky, Colonel Long had better things to do than attend ceremonies.

THIS POLITICAL SODOM

It's hard to imagine Nashville without the capitol, state office buildings and thousands of state employees—let alone the annual spectacle known as the Tennessee General Assembly. But it almost turned out differently. In fact, thanks to Nashville's reputation as a den of political iniquity, the capitol nearly ended up in some other place.

For the first few decades of Tennessee's existence, the legislature couldn't agree on a permanent capital. Knoxville was the first seat of government in 1796, followed by Nashville in 1812, Knoxville again four years later, Murfreesboro in 1819 and Nashville again seven years later. Along the way—in one of the strange footnotes of Tennessee history—Kingston served as state capital for one day in 1807.

Tennessee might have had a temporary capital for a lot longer had it not been for William Carroll, who served twelve years as governor in the 1820s and 1830s. Carroll led the fight to create a chancery court, the state's first penitentiary and the state's first insane asylum (as homes for the mentally handicapped and mentally ill were then called then).

Carroll was also largely responsible for organizing Tennessee's Constitutional Convention of 1834, a convention that debated the idea of a permanent capital at some length. Like many legislative bodies throughout history, however, it could come to no consensus and therefore decided to force other people to make the tough decision some other time: the delegates recommended (and the voters later approved) a constitutional amendment requiring the legislature to pick a permanent seat of government by 1843.

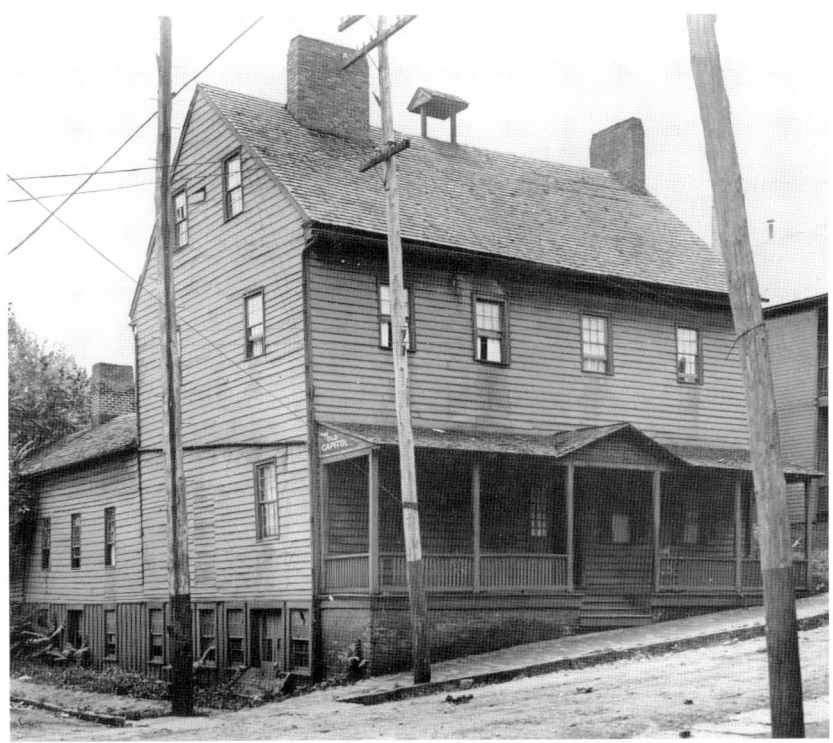

An early state capitol building in Knoxville. *Tennessee State Library and Archives.*

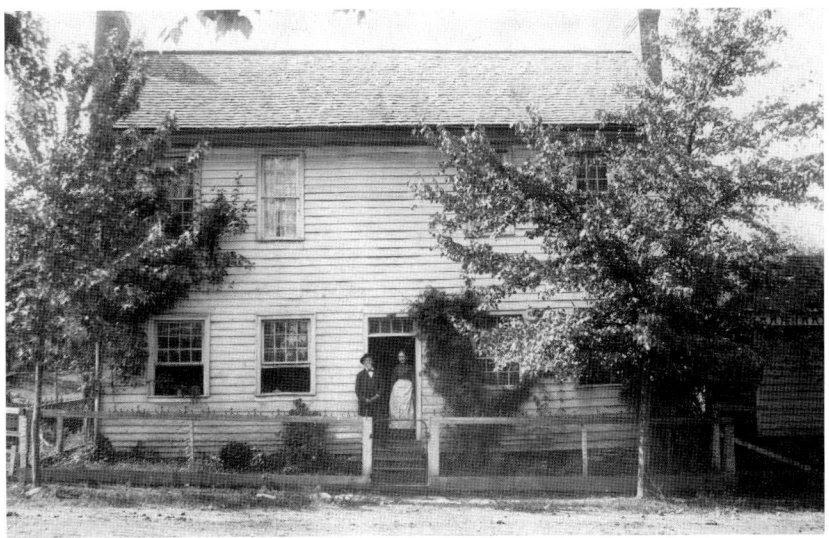

The building in Kingston that served as state capitol for a day in 1807. *Tennessee State Library and Archives.*

When the legislature met at the Davidson County Courthouse in October 1843, it spent the first week arguing over where to put the capital. House and Senate members took turns espousing the virtues of their hometowns, proposing the seat of government be placed there. Then the vote would be taken, the measure would fail and another representative or senator would stand up and espouse the virtues of his hometown.

It went on and on. Over the course of the week, just about every organized community in Tennessee got its chance and lost. During the Senate debate on the morning of October 4, Kingston, Lebanon, Hamilton, Sparta, Knoxville, Clarksville, McMinnville, Shelbyville, Murfreesboro, Chattanooga, Franklin, Harrison and Woodbury were all considered and voted down.

After lunch, the Senate considered and rejected Sparta (again), Franklin (again), Harrison (again) and Woodbury (again). Then, late on the afternoon on Wednesday, October 4, the state Senate passed a bill 13 to 12 to make Kingston the permanent capital of Tennessee.

Meanwhile, the seventy-five-member Tennessee State House was also going through a tour of Tennessee. The House version of the bill started with the seat of government located "at the centre of the state." The House then considered, and rejected, the idea of putting the capital in Nashville, Carrollville (the riverside town in Wayne County now known as Clifton), Sparta, Carthage, Nashville (again), Smithville and Murfreesboro. After a lunch break, towns suggested but voted down included Knoxville, Jackson, Carthage (again), Knoxville (again), Savannah, Jackson (again), Manchester, Murfreesboro, Lebanon, Sparta (again) and Paris. Finally, in the early evening—about the same time the Senate passed a bill to make Kingston the permanent capital—the House passed a bill making Murfreesboro the permanent capital.

That might have been an exciting night for the residents of Kingston and Murfreesboro. But the telegraph didn't exist yet, so there was no way people those communities could have known they were so close to potential glory.

On Friday the sixth, the House started up again. "The name of almost every town from Sullivan to Shelby [was] successfully proposed," the *Knoxville Post* reported. House members suggested and rejected Columbia, Harrison, Charlotte, Reynoldsburg, Shelbyville, Smithville, Manchester, Woodbury, Monticello (in Putnam County) and Chattanooga. This time, Chattanooga prevailed.

A few minutes later, the Johnson County community of Taylorsville was chosen. Then the House changed its mind yet again and picked Columbia. "These various proposals called forth some vollies of wit and several speeches, which produced a good of merriment, especially from Mr. [John] Dearing, the member from White." The House then spent the rest of the afternoon debating a measure to locate the state capital "at the most eligible point within ten miles of the geographic center of the state." Among the people who spoke in favor of this proposal was Representative William Hawkins Polk of Maury County, "a younger brother of the ex-governor, and thought by some in his party to be a more talented man" (this was obviously before James K. Polk became president).

It eventually came down to Nashville and Murfreesboro, and then, on Saturday, October 7, the debate got ugly. Several legislators said Nashville was the logical choice. After all, the legislature was used to meeting there, it had better road and water connections and it contained institutions (such as the bank and prison) that the legislature needed to keep an eye on. The City of Nashville was also offering the state a hill on which to build a capitol building. Several Nashville citizens had signed an option to buy Campbell's Hill for $30,000, acquired by attorney William Campbell years earlier as a fee for a lawsuit, to donate it to the state.

Lawmakers advocating for Murfreesboro did not go down easily. State Senator Samuel Laughlin of Warren County argued passionately against Nashville, explaining that the geographic center of the state was in Rutherford County. (In fact, at the behest of legislators from Rutherford, the state had hired a mathematician to calculate the geographic center of the state, and he had determined the location was near Murfreesboro. In 1976, the Rutherford County Historical Society paid for an obelisk to be built at this geographic center. You can find it today at 1307 Old Lascassas Road, just north of Middle Tennessee State University.)

Laughlin also noted that since the legislature moved to Nashville seventeen years earlier, the General Assembly was meeting for longer and the government had increased its annual expenditure and taken on tremendous debt. This, he said, could be attributed to the forces at work in Nashville, which he described as "this political Sodom."

State Senator William Henry Sneed, representing Rutherford and Williamson Counties, agreed with his colleague and added points of his own. "The people of Nashville are the creditor class," he said, according to the *Nashville Union*. "They were traders, speculators…while the largest portion of the people elsewhere are farmers. The interests of the two classes are averse, and their opinions of course, at variance."

Sneed made reference to Nashville's "voluptuousness" and "dissipation." He also implied that the citizens of Nashville were bribing the legislature by

STRAYED OR STOLEN,
FROM the subscriber, living on the west side of Campbell's Hill, a **RED COW,** with a white face and very long horns. She left my house about the sixteenth instant, and probably has a calf by this time. I will suitably reward any person who will bring her back if she has strayed; and if she has been stolen, I will give $20 for her return and the conviction of the thief. **W. F. BANG.**
January 26.

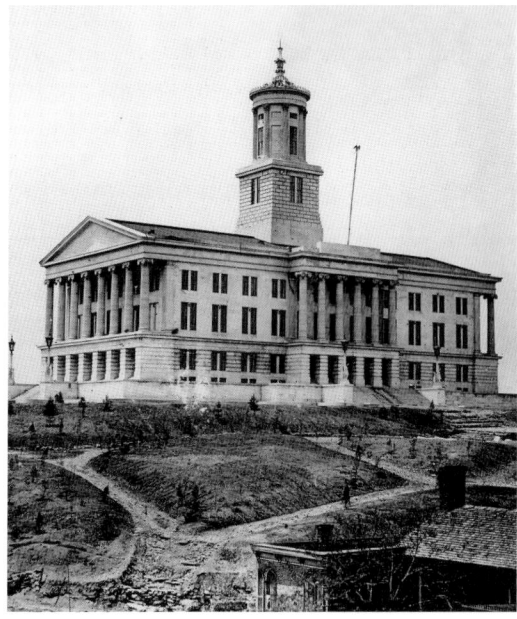

Above: Before the capitol was built, Campbell's Hill had livestock grazing on it. Nashville *Republican Banner*, January 27, 1841.

Left: The Tennessee State Capitol in 1860. *Tennessee State Library and Archives.*

offering it free land—a curious point, considering Murfreesboro was also offering the legislature free land.

That evening, the House voted 50 to 23 to make Nashville the state's permanent capital. The next day, the Senate concurred by vote of 17 to 8. Two days later, the *Republican Banner* had this to say: "The question being thus settled, let all the unpleasant circumstances connected with the conflict for the location of the Seat of Government be laid aside forever; let all thoughts of that controversy be buried in the grave of oblivion."

And what became of State Senator Sneed of Rutherford County? Two years after the state capital debate, he moved to Knoxville and set up a law practice there. One of his clients was the newly formed Hancock County—a county whose creation in 1844 had been legally challenged. Sneed represented Hancock County in that lawsuit, which went all the way to the Tennessee Supreme Court and which Hancock County won in 1848. In gratitude, the county seat, previously known as Greasy Rock, was renamed Sneedville.

Sneed was elected to Congress in 1855, on the eve of the Civil War, and was a leader in Knoxville's secessionist movement. This put him at odds with William Gannaway "Parson" Brownlow, a unionist and newspaper editor who was, in my opinion, the greatest insulter in Tennessee history. Brownlow hated Sneed so much that he publicly advocated his execution. "They [Confederate leaders in Knoxville] have filled East Tennessee with widows and orphans; they have destroyed houses and barns, fences and homes; they have plundered honest men of their stock and grain, and they have filled the land with mourning," Brownlow said of Sneed and his compatriots. "Let such imps of Hell die the deaths of traitors."

Sneed died in 1869. I don't think many people in Rutherford County, Williamson County, Roane County, Hancock County or Knox County remember him today.

LIARS, COWARDS AND POLTROONS

*I*n the old days," you may hear people say, "folks were more civil to each other." With the rise of social media, I've often heard this opinion expressed. In conversations, social media posts and even sermons, I have heard and read the notion that there was a time when people could "agree to disagree" and talk about their differences without resorting to insults.

This might be interesting if it were true. But in early Tennessee history, men insulted and attacked each other with words at least as bitter and insulting as the ones people throw at each other today. And I'm not just talking about obscure people.

The two most important men in early Tennessee history despised each other. In 1803, the hatred between Tennessee governor John Sevier and Andrew Jackson became a public spectacle. On October 26 of that year, a letter from Jackson to Sevier made its way into the *Tennessee Gazette*. "Know ye, that I, Andrew Jackson, am authorized, and do pronounce, publish and declare to the world that his excellency, John Sevier, Esquire, Governor, Captain General & Commander in Chief of the Land and Naval Forces of the State of Tennessee, is a base coward and a poltroon," Jackson wrote. "He will basely insult, but has not courage to repair the wound."

I was not familiar with the word *poltroon*, so I looked it up and learned it means "a wretched coward." I soon realized that in nineteenth-century Tennessee, men often called each other by that sobriquet. On April 25,

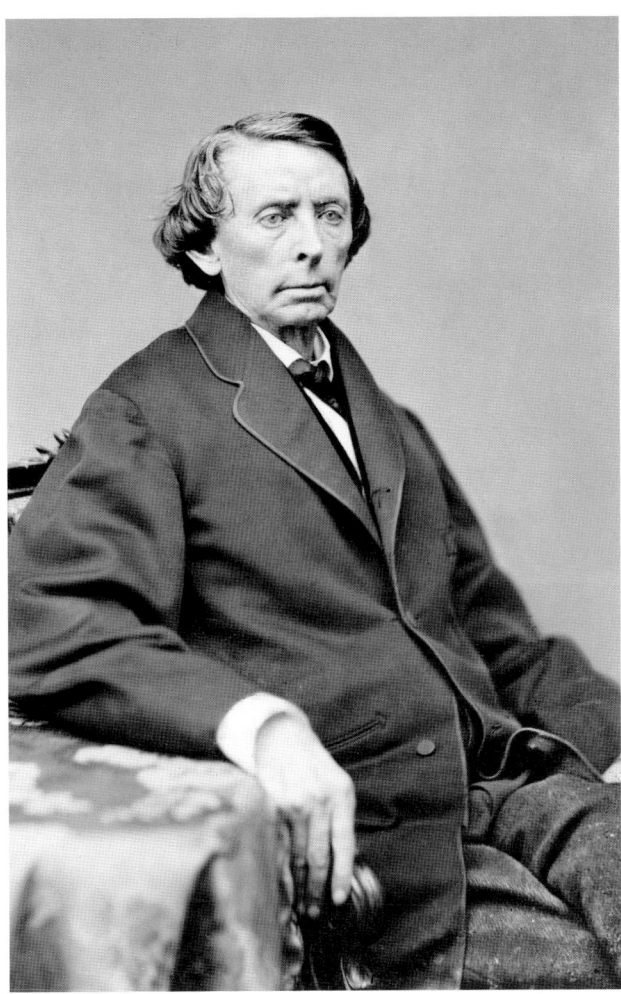

William Gannaway
Brownlow. *Mathew
Brady/Library of
Congress.*

1807, for instance, Nashville resident Edmond Saunders proclaimed
Samuel Lundy to be a "liar, coward and poltroon" in the Nashville *Impartial
Review and Cumberland Repository*.

Another prominent insulter from early Tennessee history was Thomas
Arnold, a congressman from Greeneville who counted among his enemies
Andrew Jackson, Sam Houston and James K. Polk. In January 1830, after
Polk criticized him on the floor of the U.S. House of Representatives, Arnold
sent the following message to be published in newspapers throughout the
state. "I pronounce James K. Polk of Tennessee to be a coward, a puppy, a
liar and a scoundrel generally," Arnold said. "I feel pity for his stupidity and
contempt for his servility."

However, neither Jackson nor Arnold could lay a claim to having been the greatest insulter in Tennessee history. That title would go to William Gannaway Brownlow, a Methodist minister and newspaper editor who would somehow become governor of Tennessee from 1865 to 1869. Over the course of his many years of writing editorials, Brownlow called President John Tyler a "long-eared Virginia ass," Tennessee governor James Jones a "liar," Tennessee congressman John Crozier "a dirty, mean deceitful and hateful little scoundrel" and author Harriet Beecher Stowe "as ugly as original sin…a tall, coarse, vulgar-looking woman."

Here is a sampling of Brownlow's greatest hits, published in newspapers such as *Brownlow's Whig*, the *Jonesboro Whig* and the *Knoxville Whig*:

> *I pronounce Landon Haynes of the county of Carter and state of Tennessee a liar, a puppy and a* SCOUNDREL *and if he does not call me to an account for it, the first time he comes to this village, I insist he does not possess the courage of a spaniel dog.* [January 30, 1840]

> *Point us to a female on the pavements of our streets, arm in arm with Lawson Gifford, and we will show you a female of suspicious character— or one whose family is under the weather, because of some thefts or frauds committed by the heads thereof.* [May 14, 1840]

> [Congressman Tom Anderson is] *that perjured, drunken, lying, forging, defrauding, adulterous, degraded beast, puppy and scoundrel.* [October 21, 1840)]

> *What could the people have been thinking when they elected this huge mass of corruption to Congress* [Andrew Johnson]*—this beast in human form?* [December 13, 1843]

Brownlow would also insult groups and categories of people. In the spring of 1841, he made a trip to New York City and said the people there suffer from "all sorts of diseases, mental and corporeal. Among those maladies which I have noticed the most prevalent, and the most injurious in their effects, are dizziness, restlessness at night, obstinate coughs, pains in the joints, bleeding at the nose, sore eyes, inclination to steal, headache, disposition to lie…griping of the bowels, swelling of the stomach, nausea, squeamishness, leanness, meanness, dejection of films and mums—and in short, a total want of all that is required to constitute the man."

TWO PRESIDENTS, THREE FIRST LADIES

I've run across some wonderful photographs of Tennessee history. The most interesting is property of the George Eastman Museum in Rochester, New York. The photo shows President James K. Polk posing along with a group of other people, perhaps on the lawn of the White House.

There are several things about the photo that took me aback. One is its age. The folks at the George Eastman Museum believe the photo to have been taken in either 1846 or 1847. A website called www.whitehousemuseum.org puts the date at 1849. In any case, it is one of the earliest photographs ever taken of a sitting president and possibly the first showing an American president with a group of people.

The second thing that amazes me about the photograph is the identity of the people in it. President Polk is the man on the right. To his right is his wife, Sarah Childress Polk, who would outlive her husband by forty-two years. On Polk's immediate left is Dolley Madison, widow of President James Madison. Dolley Madison was the first lady from 1809 to 1817, but by the time this photo was taken she was destitute. On the far left of the photograph is Secretary of State James Buchanan, later the fifteenth president of the United States. To Buchanan's left is Harriet Lane, Buchanan's niece, and the acting first lady during his presidency (Buchanan never married).

In other words, this photograph features two presidents and three first ladies, representing administrations that served as early as 1809 and as late as 1861.

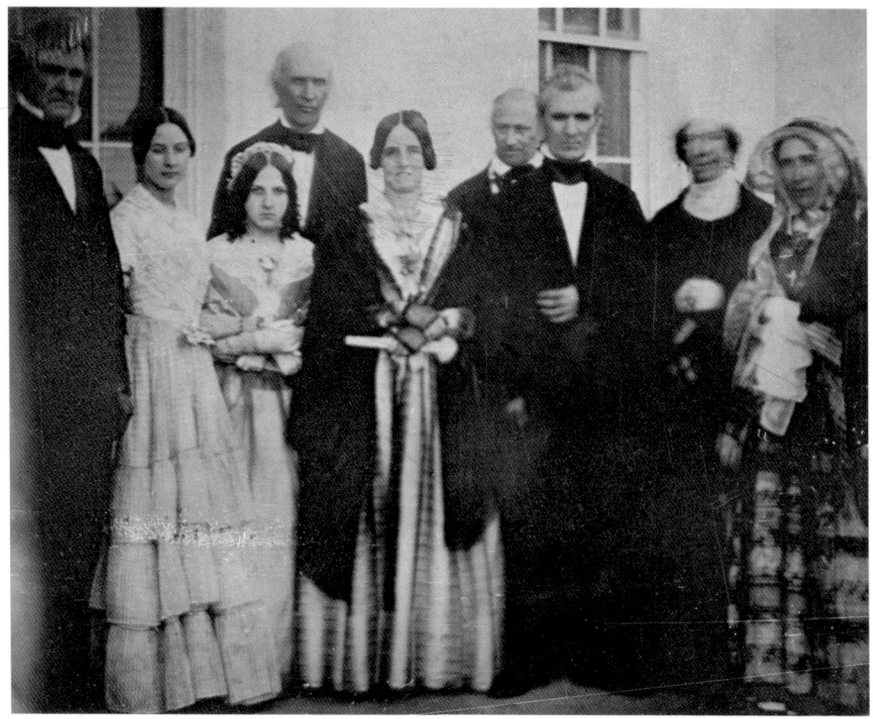

The remarkable photo of President James K. and Sarah Childress Polk, taken in 1846, 1847 or 1849. *George Eastman Museum.*

Since the image is not owned by either the Library of Congress or the Tennessee State Library and Archives, many Tennessee history experts were late in finding it. "It's an incredible photo, and I wish I had found it before now," John Seigenthaler, who wrote a book about Polk in 2003 and who died in 2014, once told me.

Besides the "big five," as I call them, I've found the remaining people in the photo to also be interesting, even though in one case we aren't sure who they are. The tall man standing in the back is Cave Johnson, postmaster general of the United States. Johnson later served as a U.S. congressman from Tennessee and is still remembered by the history buffs of Clarksville because his house is still standing there. Johnson was the postmaster when the U.S. Postal Service introduced the postage stamp in 1847. I also amuse teachers with the idea that Cave Johnson may have been the first vampire in American history (if you look at photos of the man, you will see what I mean).

The woman on the far right of the photograph is probably Cave Johnson's wife, Elizabeth Brunson Johnson. The young lady standing on Mrs. Polk's right is probably her niece Sarah Polk Rucker, who attended school in the Washington, D.C., area and frequently stayed in the White House on weekends. However, we aren't certain. Then there is the man standing behind President Polk. The cutline held by the George Eastman Museum reports this man to be Secretary of the Navy John Y. Mason. A wonderful new book called *Lady First: The World of First Lady Sarah Polk* by Amy Greenberg repeats this claim. However, the man pictured here doesn't look much like the Library of Congress photograph of Mason.

Furthermore, I've found speculation on a website called Presidential History Geeks: James K. Polk and Dolley Madison that the man standing behind Polk is Missouri senator Thomas Hart Benton. If true, this gives the photo another hook in terms of Tennessee history. After all, Thomas Hart Benton and his brother Jesse once got into a brawl with Andrew Jackson in the streets of Nashville.

Walter Borneman, author of *Polk: The Man Who Transformed the Presidency and America*, disagrees with both of these theories. "I would discount that being Thomas Hart Benton," he told me via e-mail. Borneman's alternative theory is that the man in the back might be Treasury Secretary Robert J. Walker. "He looks like a closer match than Mason." Harold Pfister's 1978 book *Facing the Light: Historic American Portrait Daguerreotypes* also identifies the man as Robert Walker. So that's two votes for Mason, one for Benton and two for Walker.

Finally, who *took* the photo? Pfister thinks the photographer was George Healy. After all, on June 16, 1946, Polk wrote this in his diary:

> *Mr. Healy, the artist, requested the cabinet and myself to go into the parlor and suffer him to take a deguerrotype likeness of the whole of us in a group. We gratified him. We found Mrs. Madison in the parlour with the ladies. Three attempts were made to take the likeness of myself, the Cabinet and the ladies in a group, all of which failed.*

As for how the group ended up outside, Healy has the following theory: "The painter, finding the parlor too dark, might have asked the company to move outdoors."

In any case, I can't help but stare at this photograph and feel some wonder that it has survived. Whether it was taken in 1846, 1847 or 1849, and whether the unidentified person is John Y. Mason, Thomas

Hart Benton, Robert J. Walker or some random man who showed up to photobomb the president and first lady, it's amazing to contemplate how much the United States would change in the twenty years after it was taken.

NED BUNTLINE'S ROPE

*H*ad the Nashville lynch mob succeeded, American history might have turned out differently. There might not have been a "Know Nothing" political movement. There might not have been a "Buffalo" Bill Cody, at least not in the eyes of the public. In fact, the image of the American West might have been different had someone—maybe the mayor—not cut the rope that would have hanged Edward Zane Carroll Judson in front of the Nashville courthouse.

As luck would have it, however, Judson survived the attempt on his life, although his brush with a group of angry Nashvillians crippled him for the rest of his days.

Judson was better known by the pen name Ned Buntline. Author, journalist, activist, self-promoter and showman, he was famous for different things at different times of his life. There's all sorts of information about Buntline at the Buffalo Bill Center of the West in Cody, Wyoming. "Poor people read his [Buntline's] books and wanted to go West," a 1951 book about him claims.

Buntline's name even turns up on weaponry (Colt once allegedly produced a revolver with a twelve-inch barrel known as the "Buntline Special") and in Mark Twain novels (at one point, Tom Sawyer pretended to be in one of Buntline's pirate novels).

Judson was born in 1821 in Upstate New York. At seventeen, while a midshipman in the navy, he wrote a story for a national magazine called *The Knickerbocker*. He gave himself the pen name Ned Buntline (the word *buntline* is a nautical term referring to the rope at the bottom of a square sail). Other stories followed, and he found an audience for his tales about pirates and other adventures at sea. When Judson got out of the navy, he started his own publication called *Ned Buntline's Magazine.* People read it, but it later folded, as did two successor publications.

In 1845, Judson and his wife, Seberina, moved to Nashville. Apparently, they were drawn there for two reasons. One was cultural: at the time, Nashville was the political center of what was still, culturally at least, the American West. The other reason was personal: Judson had a personal connection to *Nashville Banner* editor Felix Zollicoffer.

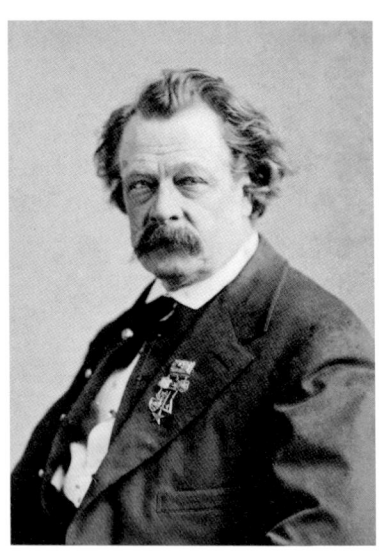

Edward Zane Carroll Judson, aka Ned Buntline.

A man who married seven times, Edward Zane Carroll Judson always did have a way with the ladies. During his short stint in Nashville, he allegedly got involved with someone else's. At the time, one of the prettiest women in town was Mary Porterfield, the teenage wife of an auctioneer named Robert Porterfield. Married or not, Judson was quite the figure around town and apparently caught her eye.

In details that later came out in court, Judson started to woo the young lady—by talking to her and, on at least one occasion, sending her a short poem. Rumors persisted about the two of them at the Trabue boardinghouse, which is where young Mr. and Mrs. Porterfield were living at the time. Judson and Mrs. Porterfield were seen together in suspicious circumstances—once in an alley beside a church.

Finally, Robert Porterfield met Judson and warned him to stay away from his wife. The warning apparently went unheeded because a few days later, on March 11, 1846, a minister spotted Judson and Mrs. Porterfield together in the graveyard in which the Porterfields' infant daughter had been buried. They were "standing face to face very near each other and apparently engaged in close conversation," the minister later testified.

A few nights later, Porterfield found Judson and started shooting at him. Judson fired back and struck Porterfield with a bullet right above his eye. Hours later, Buntline gave himself up to the local sheriff.

In those days, law and order were relative concepts. When the hearing took place, Porterfield's brother barged into the courtroom and opened fire on the accused. Judson fled the courthouse and into the City Hotel across the street. A mob dragged him to jail.

That night, Robert Porterfield died of his wound. The mob reassembled, and as an eyewitness later said (referring to Judson as "Buntline"):

> *When the mob rushed into the jail they knocked* [the jailer Louis] *Hord out of a rocking chair and secured the keys when he said "For God's sake, don't let all the prisoners out." Three of the mob entered Buntline's cell. While one caught him by a leg another seized him by the collar. A third, placing his foot on Buntline's neck, was about to fire when the jailer pleaded with him not to kill him there. Buntline was then dragged pell-mell into the street. He was then permitted to say his prayers, and on finishing pulled a ring from his finger, handed it to a minister to be sent to his father at Pittsburgh. The crowd then halloed, "take him on," and they did so.*

A rope was tied around Judson's neck, and he was hanged from an awning post on a public square. Before his neck broke, however, the rope snapped, and his body tumbled back to the ground. "The rope was cut by a friend," Judson later wrote. (An 1886 account of the incident claimed that Nashville mayor S.V.D. Stout cut the rope; perhaps Stout was the "friend" to whom Judson referred.)

A few days later, after order had been restored, the grand jury absolved Judson from any crimes. He left town immediately and never stepped foot in Tennessee again. The widow Porterfield's troubles continued; the next year, after a lengthy and well-publicized public hearing, she was excommunicated from the Baptist Church.

Incredibly, Judson's Nashville adventure fits in with the rest of his life. After escaping death, he moved to New York and began writing popular fiction, most notably a series of stories dramatizing the squalid living conditions of the working-class people of New York (a prelude to the books of Upton Sinclair three quarters of a century later). He also started his own muckraking newspaper, *Ned Buntline's Own*, and used it to publish his own stories and advance his causes, which by now included prohibition, suspicion of foreigners and Catholics and reform politics.

Somewhere along the line, the man became publicly known as Ned Buntline; most public references to "Edward Z.C. Judson" cease (I suppose it was too much trouble to write). In any case, around 1854, Buntline was credited (at least in one New York newspaper) with starting the political party now known as the Know Nothing Party. "The Know Nothing Party, it is pretty generally known, was first formed by a person of some notoriety who called himself 'Ned Buntline,'" the *New York Daily Times* reported. "Ned instructed his proselytes and acolytes to reply to all questions in respect to the movements of the new party, 'I don't know.' So they were at first called 'Don't-Knows,' and then 'Know-Nothings' by outsiders, who knew nothing more of them than that they invariably replied 'I don't know' to all questions." The Know Nothing Party was a notable factor in American politics but largely dissolved in 1856.

As busy and prominent as he was, however, Buntline was never out of trouble for long. With each exposé and crusade, he took on new enemies. He was twice convicted for starting riots, first in New York and later in St. Louis. In 1854, he shot and killed an African American man but was later acquitted of murder on grounds of self-defense. And as far as his being a leader in the temperance movement, he might make a speech or two, "but only after he'd braced himself with a few drinks," one account of his life claims.

Buntline was a soldier in the U.S. Army in the Civil War, enlisting as a private with the New York militia. It was, curiously enough, the most uneventful part of his life; he spent a year in Northern Virginia, saw little combat and was discharged because of injury. (None of this stopped him from lying about his military career; he was often referred to as "Colonel Judson" in later years.)

After the war, Buntline focused his career on writing dime-store novels with names such as *The Comanche's Dream* and *King of the Border Men*. Here he found his literary niche. Buntline wrote more than four hundred novels, scribbling chapters on trains, in hotel rooms and whenever he needed the money and could find the time. During the years following the Civil War, he may have been the highest-paid writer in America. Many people first learned about the American West by reading Buntline's novels, which were inspired by real-life events but certainly not accurate depictions of the West.

In 1869, on a trip through the West, Buntline met Bill Cody, a trapper, former Pony Express rider and scout. Many of Cody's friends were already beginning to call him "Buffalo Bill," but it was a story written by Buntline in the *New York Weekly* that made Cody's nickname a household phrase.

A few years later, Buntline wrote a stage production called *The Scouts of the Plains*, featuring himself, Cody and "Texas Jack" Omohundro, another scout and hero of the Old West. The play launched Cody's stage career (not Buntline's, as Ned was a poor actor with a bad back, injured all those years

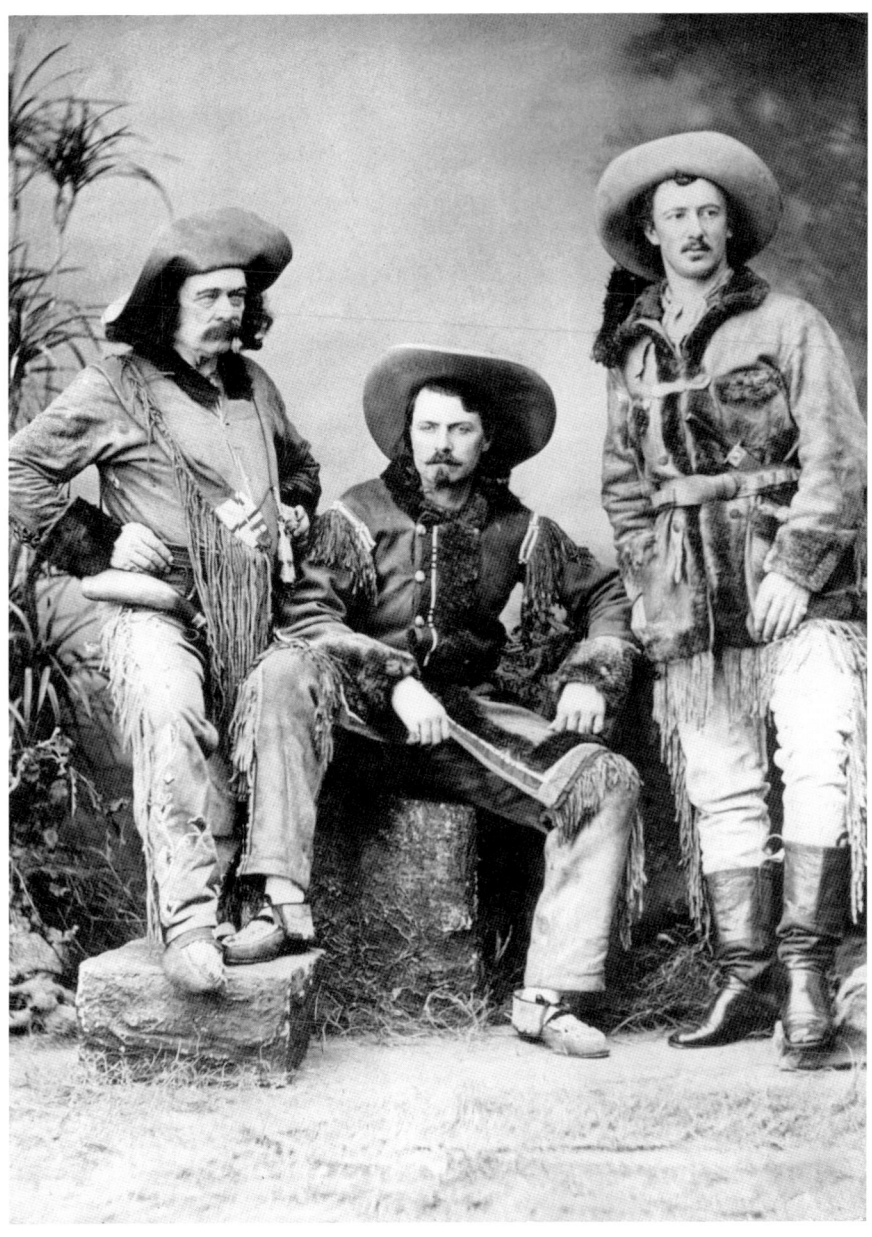

Ned Buntline, Buffalo Bill Cody and Texas Jack Omohundro in 1872. *Buffalo Bill Center, Harold McCracken Research Library.*

earlier while trying to escape the Nashville lynch mob). In 1887, Buffalo Bill's Wild West Show hit the stage, starring real cowboys and real Native Americans but not Ned Buntline. The show spent ten of its thirty years in Europe and turned "Buffalo Bill" Cody into one of the most famous men in the world.

Buntline eventually returned to New York and remained a celebrity for his later years, frequently granting interviews. However, he was rarely asked about his near brush with the Nashville lynch mob. When he died in 1886, practically every newspaper in America contained a lengthy obituary of the man, some of them replete with exaggerations and tall tales. "Ned Buntline probably carried more wounds in his body than any living American," claimed one version of his obituary, which was published in dozens of papers. "He had in his right knee a bullet received in Virginia and had twelve other wounds inflicted by sword, shell and gun, even or which were got in battle."

Another claim: "His father was a Philadelphia lawyer, who insisted upon putting Ned through a course of Latin and Blackstone at an early age. The boy rebelled, and one day, after a severe flogging, ran away to sea as a cabin boy to a ship that sailed round the Horn. The embryo celebrity was then but eleven years old."

Another claim: "He once earned $12,500 in six weeks, and at another time, under pressure, wrote a book of 610 pages in sixty-two hours, scarcely sleeping or eating during that time."

Truth or not, hundreds attended the funeral of Edward Zane Carroll Judson. A few days later, two different women came forward, each claiming to be his wife and entitled to his estate.

BRITANNIA ARRIVES AT BOSTON

On Monday, March 6, 1848, people walked around Nashville excitedly blurting out the same sentence: "Did you hear the *Britannia* arrived at Boston?" It was an unusual greeting. After all, no one in Tennessee probably cared about the steamship *Britannia*. The important thing was that the *Britannia* had arrived in Boston only two days before. The fact that the *news* was *new* is what made people so excited.

The news of the *Britannia* was the first information ever transmitted to Nashville by telegraph—the first news ever received in Tennessee that had not come by foot, horse or boat. Before March 6, 1848, it could take as long as three weeks for news to get from New York or Washington, D.C., to Nashville.

To understand the telegraph, you have to go back to another steamship voyage sixteen years earlier. On a voyage from Great Britain to New York in 1832, a painter named Samuel Morse and a doctor named Charles Thomas Jackson had several long talks about electricity.

People had known about electricity for years. Benjamin Franklin had conducted experiments with it eighty years earlier. But no one had found a way to really *use* it. During their long talks, Morse and Jackson talked about whether an electrical current—if created, broken, then created and broken again and again in a series of patterns—could be used for long-distance communication.

Morse was so excited when he got to New York that he started doing experiments with electricity. But he wasn't the only man working on it. Other scientists were already trying to find a way to use electricity to communicate long distance, which is why we can't really call Morse the sole "inventor" of the telegraph. What Morse eventually did, along with the help of Leonard Gale and Alfred Vail, was come up with a series of circuits and relays that enabled the telegraph to send messages long distances.

On January 6, 1838, Morse and Vail demonstrated their invention by sending a message along two miles of electric wire at the Speedwell Ironworks in Morristown, New Jersey.

You might assume that this demonstration would have gotten everyone's attention, but it didn't. A message sent along a two-mile-long wire was one thing, but people still didn't think you could send a message twenty or thirty miles. To demonstrate that, Morse needed a lot of money, which he didn't have. He also needed help from the government.

You see, back then, you couldn't just string twenty miles of wire from one place to another unless you owned a twenty-mile-long strip of land. But the federal government didn't pay for or even allow this sort of thing in 1838. There was nothing in the U.S. Constitution about a person having the right to string telegraph lines all over the place, which is why members of Congress scratched their heads when Morse asked them to help him.

In 1843, the U.S. House of Representatives voted 89 to 80 to allocate $30,000 and give Morse the legal right to string a telegraph line a long distance. Morse and his friends got to work, laying a telegraph line along the way from Washington, D.C., to Baltimore.

It wasn't easy. After all, copper wires were hard to come by, and thirty-eight miles of copper wire, well, just didn't exist. A company had to be hired to make the wire, long poles had to be purchased to hold the wire and men had to be paid to stick the poles in the ground and string the wire to the top of them. This took time and patience, and Morse's mood was up one minute and down the next. "He changes oftener than the wind," Vail said. "Now he is elated up to the skies, then he is down in the mud."

On May 25, 1844, a group of businessmen and elected officials gathered around a funny-looking electronic device in the Capitol in Washington, while another group of men gathered around another funny-looking electronic device at a railroad office in Baltimore. Morse, at one end, typed in a series of dots and dashes into a machine that would have looked, to us, like a cross between a stapler and a small cash register. Vail, forty miles away and on the other end the wire, translated the dots and dashes into a four-word message.

The letters dots and dashes came one at a time, and Vail translated them, using the code he and Morse had come up with. The first letter was *w*. The

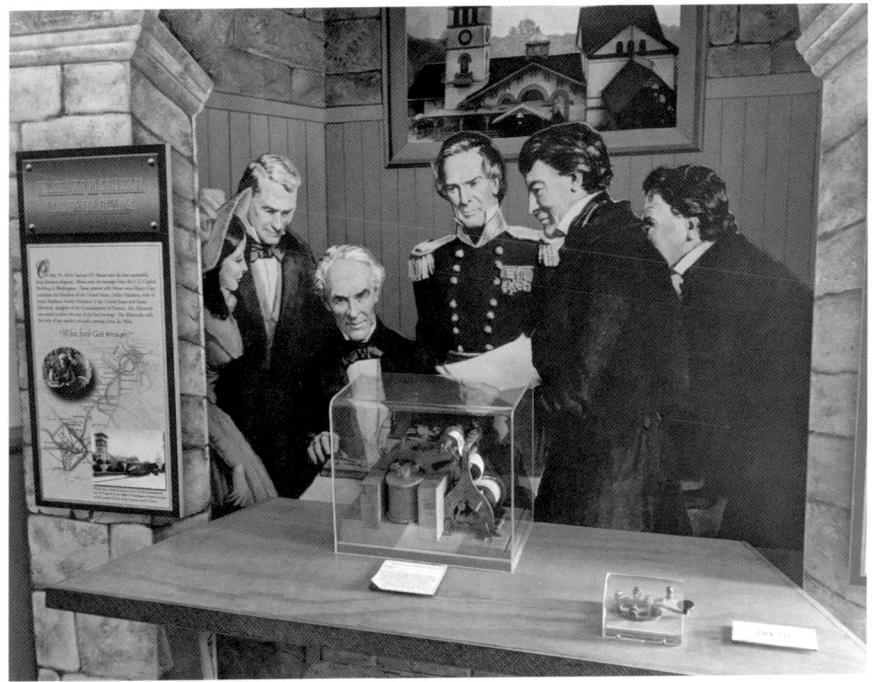

A diorama at the B&O Railroad Museum in Baltimore. *Author's collection.*

second was *h*. The third was *a*. And so on. Vail transcribed the message one letter at a time. It spelled out the words "What hath God wrought"—a Bible verse (Numbers 23:23) that a girl had chosen for Morse. The men standing around Vail, at the railroad office in Baltimore, were amazed. "Send him something in return!" they probably said. "No, no…send him a question! See if he can respond to a question." Newspaper reporters realized the implications of what Morse and Vail had done. "Time and space have been completely annihilated," said the *Baltimore Sun*.

Morse now had the world's attention and as many investors as he needed. He and his partners formed a business called the Magnetic Telegraph Company to build telegraph lines to New York City, Philadelphia, Boston, Buffalo and other large cities. Morse would also sign an agreement with a man named Henry O'Reilly, who started another business called the Atlantic & Ohio Telegraph Company. It was this company—the Atlantic & Ohio—that extended telegraph lines to Cincinnati, Ohio; Louisville, Kentucky; and Nashville.

The lines were installed at the rate of about ten miles per day through Kentucky, heading south from Louisville. O'Reilly and his crew showed up

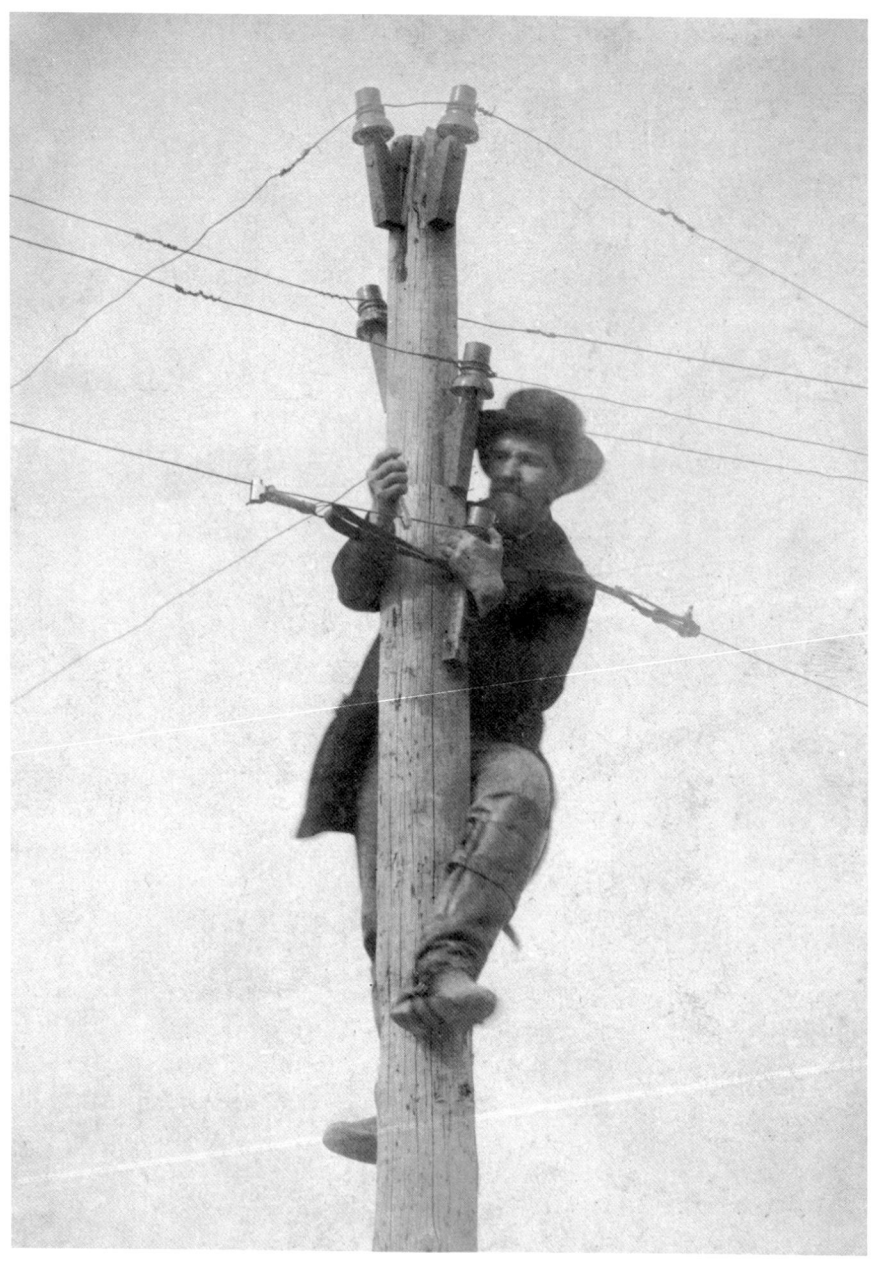

A man installing telegraph wire in the 1880s. *Library of Congress.*

in Nashville on or about Tuesday, February 24, 1848, sticking poles in the ground and attaching wire to the top of them as fast as they could. It took a few days to get the apparatus working.

So it was that, on March 6, 1848, the *Nashville Daily Union* reported that the steamboat *Britannia* had arrived in Boston—a bit of news no one cared about but everyone talked about. Since then, news has made its way instantly into Tennessee—via telegraph, later by telephone, later by television and later by internet.

Finally, a postscript about Morse and O'Reilly: By the time the telegraph arrived in Nashville, the partnership between the two men had become a rivalry and a lawsuit. That case (*O'Reilly v. Morse*) made it all the way to the U.S. Supreme Court. In January 1854, the high court ruled in Morse's favor, causing the collapse of O'Reilly's business empire. When O'Reilly died in 1886, newspapers in Tennessee made a small mention of it, saying he had been a prominent citizen of Rochester, New York. But no one pointed out that it was O'Reilly who had brought the telegraph to Tennessee.

PRESIDENT LEAVES A MESS OF A LEGACY

*J*ames K. Polk accomplished much during his four-year term as America's eleventh president. He acquired more than 1 million square miles of land for the United States. He lowered the tariff on imported goods. He oversaw the process under which the first U.S. postage stamp was issued. The U.S. government formed a naval academy.

In fact, historians today consider Polk to have been the last "strong" American president before the Civil War. President Polk was unsuccessful, however, in leaving a permanent monument to his life.

Polk is one of three Tennesseans who became president (along with Andrew Jackson and Andrew Johnson). Like the other two, Polk wasn't actually born in the Volunteer State. Polk was born in a log cabin near the present-day site of Charlotte, North Carolina. He was the first of ten children born to Samuel Polk, who made his living as a land surveyor. When James was ten years old, Samuel Polk migrated to Middle Tennessee, settling near present-day Columbia.

Samuel Polk was successful in Maury County; at a time when land was being subdivided for the first time, there was plenty of work for a surveyor.

Samuel Polk sent his son James to the University of North Carolina, from which he graduated at the top of his class. (In fact, it was then, when James was the president of student body at the University of North Carolina, that his name first appeared in the newspaper.) Returning to Tennessee, James Polk became apprenticed to prominent Nashville attorney Felix Grundy. Grundy introduced Polk to some of the most important people in Nashville, including Andrew Jackson. He also probably helped young James become clerk of the Tennessee Senate—a part-time gig, admittedly, but a wonderful introduction to politics for a young lawyer.

By 1820, James Polk was ready to practice law, but not ready to live alone. He moved back home with his parents, who by this time had a prominent residence two blocks from the Maury County Courthouse in Columbia. Today, this house is still standing; it's known as the Polk Ancestral Home and is open to the public. Polk lived in this house with his parents and many of his brothers and sisters, although it is believed he traveled frequently as part of his job to nearby county seats such as Lawrenceburg, Murfreesboro and Shelbyville.

In those days (long before television, radio and the internet), court proceedings were popular entertainment; many people went to see them and became familiar with the lawyers on both sides. Young, intelligent, good-looking James K. Polk made a name for himself, and in 1823, he ran for the Tennessee State House and defeated the incumbent.

At that time, Murfreesboro was the capital of Tennessee. And although we aren't certain about how the two originally met, James Polk courted and married Sarah Childress of Murfreesboro while he served in the legislature there. Only a few years later, in 1825, Polk successfully ran for a seat in the U.S. House of Representatives.

Polk would remain a member of the U.S. House of Representatives for fourteen years—the last four as the Speaker of the House. As a legislator, Polk was generally supportive of Jacksonian Democracy, which meant he was opposed to the central bank, preferred agricultural interests to industrial interests, favored the Indian Removal Act of 1830 and supported westward expansion. (These positions earned him the nickname "Young Hickory," in reference to Jackson's status as "Old Hickory.")

Polk left Congress in 1839 and successfully ran for governor of Tennessee. However, he lost the governor's race in 1841 and 1843 as the Democratic Party lost ground in Tennessee to the Whig Party.

Then came one of the most memorable presidential elections of all time. At the Democratic National Convention in 1844, Polk was nominated for president on the ninth ballot, becoming the first "dark horse" candidate to be nominated by a major political party in the United States. That fall, Polk successfully ran against Whig Henry Clay with a campaign slogan "54-40 or fight!" in reference to an ongoing border dispute with Canada.

President Polk had a very active four-year term. Through diplomatic efforts, he acquired from Great Britain the land that now comprises all the states of Washington, Oregon, Idaho and parts of Montana and Wyoming. After his attempts to acquire California through negotiation with Mexico failed, the United States ended up at war with its southern neighbor. It was a lopsided and short war, and when it was over, Mexico ceded the modern-day states of California, Nevada, Utah, Arizona and parts of the states of New Mexico, Colorado and Wyoming.

Polk chose not to run for reelection and, at fifty three, was the youngest former president in U.S. history. He looked forward to retiring at Polk Place, a home in the heart of Nashville that he and his wife had acquired years earlier from his former mentor, Felix Grundy.

It was not to be. On June 15, 1849—only 103 days after leaving office— Polk died of cholera during an epidemic in Nashville. At first his body was buried in a mass grave for cholera victims in Nashville's City Cemetery, but it was later moved to a grave in the front yard of Polk Place.

Sarah Childress Polk wore black (to show she was in mourning) for the rest of her life. But she lived on and remained one of Nashville's most highly respected citizens for the next forty-two years. Polk Place and Mrs. Polk were revered by people from every political persuasion. During the Civil War, Polk Place was considered neutral ground by both the Confederate

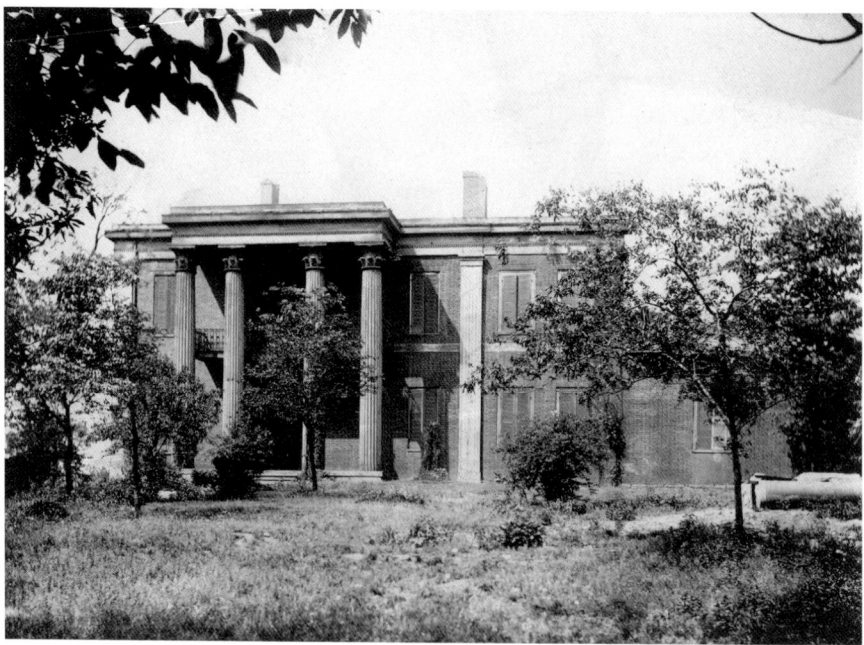

Polk Place. *Tennessee State Library and Archives.*

and Union armies. In spite of the fact that she had nephews fighting on the Confederate side, Union generals Don Carlos Buell and Ulysses S. Grant paid their respects to the former first lady. Mrs. Polk didn't venture out much, other than attending weekly church services at the First Presbyterian Church three blocks away (where a pew still bears her name).

Meanwhile, like everyone else whose income was dependent on the labor of enslaved people, Mrs. Polk had no real income after the Civil War; in those days, there was no retirement fund for former first ladies. The state came to her aid in February 1870, taking Polk Place off the property tax rolls "so long as Mrs. Polk may live and occupy the premises as a place of residence." In exchange for this privilege, Mrs. Polk made it a tradition to host the Tennessee General Assembly after it adjourned every year. In fact, many out-of-town visitors to Nashville would stop in and see Mrs. Polk and were astounded at just how friendly she was. "I see you are a stranger, sir, but happy to see you, nevertheless," she told a visitor to Nashville in 1876. "People call every day to see me to see how a woman lives that lived in the White House once, and I value the attention very highly."

Sarah Childress Polk died in 1891. What followed was a legal dispute centered on James K. Polk's will, and eventually the will was declared invalid. The State of Tennessee nearly acquired Polk Place and made it the governor's mansion (at the time, the governor of Tennessee lived in a hotel room). But that did not occur; instead, on September 19, 1893, the state had the graves of President and Mrs. Polk exhumed and moved to the grounds of the Tennessee Capitol.

Another several years of argument ensued, during which the Polk Place mansion fell into disrepair. Then, on February 5, 1898, the Davidson County Chancery Court auctioned the Polk Place home and grounds for $15,000.

The land ended up in the hands of developer J. Craig McClanahan, who tore down the mansion and built an apartment building on the site. If you are looking for the date of the razing—the moment in time when (in my opinion) the worst architectural crime in Tennessee history took place—I would estimate that date as the first of December 1900. That week, an advertisement appeared on page five of the *Nashville American*. "FOR SALE," the ad claimed. "Building stone for sale cheap at old Polk Place. Apply at once." In other words, the Polk Place mansion survived the Civil War only to be torn down so an apartment building could be built on the site.

All of this makes President James K. Polk, one of the most successful presidents in American history, the only president whose body has been dug up and moved twice. Today, however, the spot in which he and Mrs. Polk are buried is one of the most peaceful in downtown Nashville. If you walk around to the northeast side of the state capitol, you will see the grave. It's a good place to sit and contemplate the president who deserved more respect than he got.

TENNESSEE'S CONNECTION TO *UNCLE TOM'S CABIN*

*I*t's hard to overstate the importance of the novel *Uncle Tom's Cabin*. It was second-best-selling book of the nineteenth century (following the Bible) and had been translated into twenty languages by 1857, which was remarkable for its time. Harriet Beecher Stowe's book had a profound effect on the abolitionist movement and on the way average Americans viewed slavery. In fact, it has been widely reported that Abraham Lincoln, upon being introduced to Stowe in 1862, said she was "the little woman who wrote the book that started this great war."

In Tennessee, public school teachers are supposed to talk about the Civil War in grades 4 and 8, and specifically about the Tennessee battles of the Civil War in the standalone semester of Tennessee history in grade 5. However, there isn't really a connection between Tennessee and *Uncle Tom's Cabin*, is there? Actually, there is. But for 170 years, the world of Tennessee history has deliberately avoided it.

Richard Dillingham (born in 1823) was a Quaker teacher from near Cincinnati, Ohio, who knew some free African Americans who had relatives held in slavery in Nashville. In December 1848, he came to Nashville and tried to help these enslaved people escape. Dillingham was caught and jailed on December 7, 1848.

From its tone, the Nashville *Republican Banner* had no sympathy for the man: "A man who calls himself Dillingham was arrested in this city on Tuesday night by Constable [William] Maddux, in the act of kidnapping a number of slaves. He had them in a hack and was about crossing the

CHOLERA.

We regret to learn that the Cholera is rather on the increase in this vicinity. On Sunday there were some sixty cases of cholera and diarrhœa at the Penitentiary and one death, the deceased, a man named Dillingham, (put in for attempting to run off negroes,) having been attacked about breakfast time, died, and was buried at half past three P. M. The malignity of the disease appears without precedent. We learn that a large number have been attacked on the opposite side of the river, many cases of which have proved fatal. This is a sad condition of things.

Nashville *Republican Banner,* July 2, 1850.

bridge. This is a curious transaction for this latitude, as he could hardly expect one would suppose to get them off to a free state unmolested. He is in custody."

Four months later, Dillingham was sentenced to three years in the state penitentiary, which was then located near the present-day site of Charlotte and Fifteenth Avenues in Nashville. Nashville's largest newspapers endorsed his sentence, with the *Nashville Daily Union* saying, "We seriously doubt the policy of extending to such violations of the law very great lenity."

Dillingham died a year and a half later, still in prison. "We regret to learn that the Cholera is rather on the increase in this vicinity," the *Republican Banner* reported on July 2, 1850. "On Sunday there were some sixty cases of cholera and diarrhea at the penitentiary and one death, the deceased, a man named Dillingham (put in for attempting to run off negroes)."

Dillingham was buried at the prison cemetery, which means his remains lie in an unmarked grave somewhere near the corner of Fifteenth Avenue and Charlotte (near a Burger King, as best I can tell).

Dillingham's case was well publicized at the time. News of his arrest was reported as far away as England, and news of his death appeared in abolitionist publications all over the North. He was considered a martyr by people such as John Greenleaf Whittier, who wrote a poem in his honor. Prominent Quaker and abolitionist Levi Coffin wrote about Dillingham in his memoirs.

A year after Dillingham's death, Harriet Beecher Stowe came out with *Uncle Tom's Cabin.* In the months following its publication, many southern politicians, editors and ministers claimed she deliberately exaggerated the horrors of slavery in her novel. That's why, in 1853, she published *A Key to Uncle Tom's Cabin*—a list of people, facts and events on which *Uncle Tom's Cabin* was based.

Chapter 13 of *A Key to Uncle Tom's Cabin* is about Quaker abolitionists who were active in the Underground Railroad. Much of this chapter is devoted to the story of Richard Dillingham, the twenty-five-year-old Quaker from Morrow County, Ohio, who was arrested in Tennessee for trying to help slaves escape and who died in prison a year later.

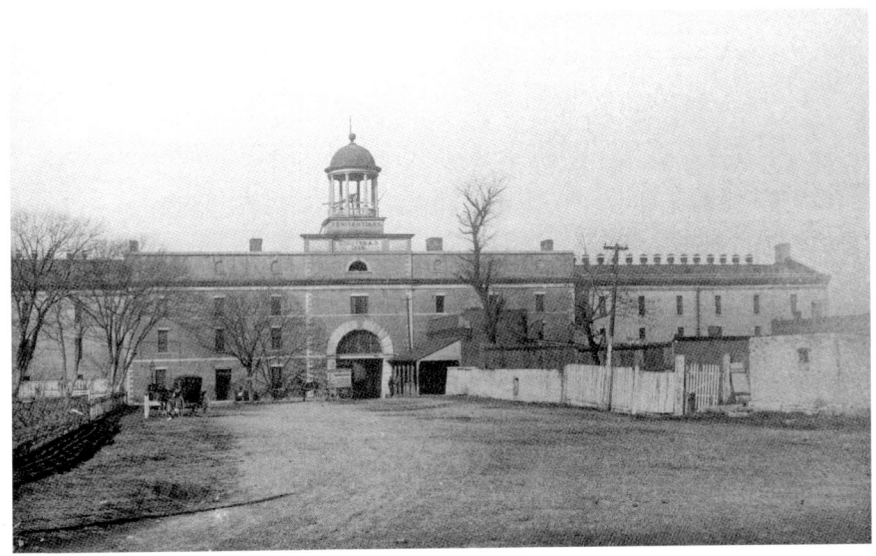

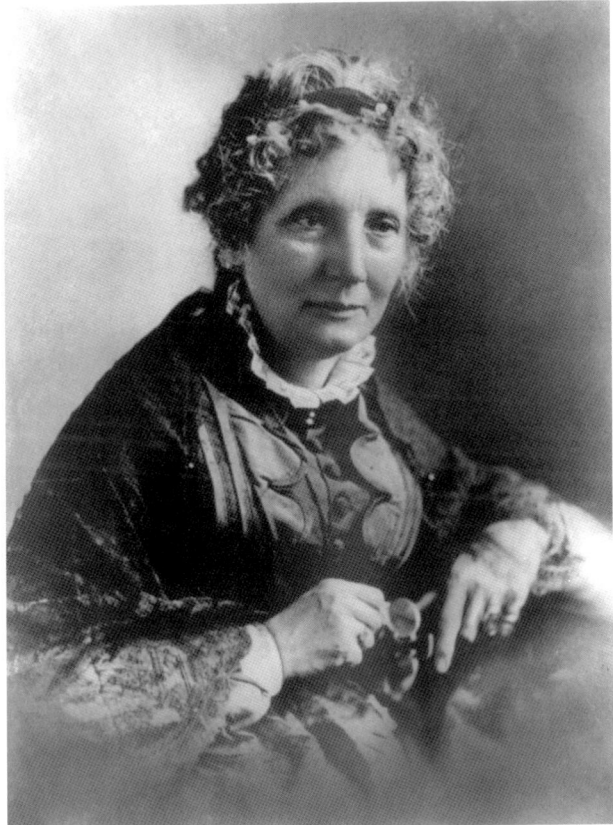

Above: The Tennessee
State Penitentiary.
*Tennessee State Library and
Archives.*

Left: Harriet Beecher
Stowe. *Schlesinger Library,
Harvard University.*

Stowe maintained that Dillingham's mother pleaded with Tennessee governor Neill Brown to pardon her son, to no avail. Stowe also claimed that Dillingham was working in the prison infirmary, tending other sick inmates when cholera broke out. "What must that system be which makes it necessary to imprison with convicted felons a man like this, because he loves his brother man 'not wisely but too well?'" Stowe wrote.

The story of Richard Dillingham affected the abolitionist movement and was one of the many things that inspired Harriet Beecher Stowe to write *Uncle Tom's Cabin*. My question is this: Why isn't Dillingham a part of Tennessee history? Why isn't he mentioned in the *Tennessee Encyclopedia of History and Culture*? And why on earth isn't there a historic marker honoring him at the former site of the Tennessee State Prison?

NASHVILLE NATIVE INVADES NICARAGUA

During the first half of the nineteenth century, enormous chunks of land were annexed by the United States, some of it by purchase (the Louisiana Purchase, for example) and some of it through war (California and New Mexico, for example). Americans who lived then didn't know when it would end.

By the 1840s, many Americans believed their nation should expand to the South and take over places such as Cuba and Nicaragua. Some went so far as to organize independent armies that invaded these countries with hopes of becoming rich and expanding the boundaries of the United States. These people were known as filibusters, and the most famous of them was a Nashville native named William Walker.

As a young man, Walker spent two years in France and then moved to New Orleans, where he worked as a newspaper editor. There he fell in love with a deaf young lady in New Orleans and was devastated when she died in the cholera epidemic of 1849 (the same epidemic that killed James K. Polk).

After her death, Walker moved to San Francisco and became convinced he would do something important in his life. In 1853, he raised an army of forty-five people—"reckless saloon loafers and the dregs of the California docks," one of his biographies claims—and took them on a ship to invade the area then known as Lower California and Sonora, Mexico. His group had a few minor military victories and took over the town of La Paz. The Mexican army forced him to retreat, and after he was back in California, he was tried as a criminal for conducting an illegal war.

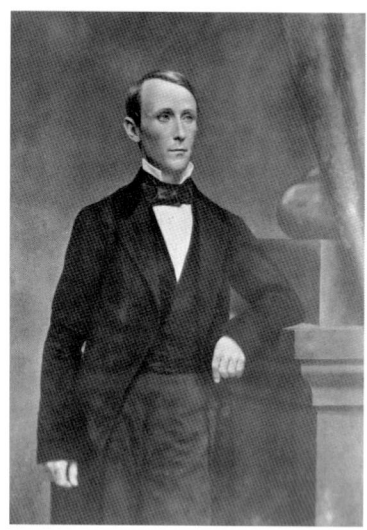

William Walker. *Library of Congress.*

Walker was acquitted, and some of the land his men had been fighting for was acquired by the United States in what became known as the Gadsden Purchase. To this day, no one knows whether Walker's Mexican excursion had anything to do with Mexico's willingness to part with that land. But at the time, people believed Walker and his invasion were factors. He was, in the minds of many people, a hero.

About this time, Americans were especially interested in Nicaragua. Starting with the discovery of gold in California in 1849, thousands of Americans moved west. But there was no transcontinental railroad and no Panama Canal yet. The quickest and least expensive way from the East Coast to San Francisco was to take a ship from New York to Nicaragua, a boat up the San Juan River and then across to Lake Nicaragua, a stagecoach across a twelve-mile strip of land in western Nicaragua and a ship to San Francisco.

This route was controlled by Cornelius Vanderbilt, one of the most powerful men in America at that time. Vanderbilt and other Americans weren't sure what to make of Nicaragua and its government, which had been independent from Spain since 1821 but had experienced a dozen revolutions since then.

In 1854, civil war broke out in Nicaragua. One of the political parties asked Walker for support, and in May 1855, he sailed from San Francisco with fifty-eight armed men. They landed a few weeks later on the west coast of Nicaragua, and within months, his army had effectively taken over the nation.

Early on, there were indications that the Nicaraguan people might embrace Walker. Among the Native American peoples of Nicaragua, there had been a legend that a "gray-eyed stranger" would come to their shores and become their leader. William Walker began calling himself the "gray-eyed man of destiny." He declared English the official language of Nicaragua, made slavery legal and began to work toward a long-term goal of making it a part of the United States.

But in 1855 and 1856, several things happened that brought an end to his short reign. In the summer of 1855, he made peace with the leader of the opposition party, General Ponciano Corral, but a few months later accused him of treason and had him publicly executed, which turned many Nicaraguans against Walker.

Walker's success concerned the governments of the other Central American nations, who feared that his army would eventually invade neighboring countries in an attempt to turn Central America into a series of American colonies.

Rather than ally himself with Vanderbilt, Walker also made the mistake of taking Vanderbilt's transit business away from him. Vanderbilt effectively created a blockade of that country, sent money and arms to help defeat Walker, used his newspapers to crusade against Walker and took steps to make certain the American government did nothing to help him.

Vanderbilt teamed up with Costa Rican president Juan Rafael Mora Porras and sent an army to attack Walker. A short war followed. And although all of the battles involving Walker and his army seem like skirmishes compared to the American Civil War that took place shortly thereafter, people in Central America remember them well.

For instance, at the Battle of Hacienda San Jacinto, a Nicaraguan named Andres Castro turned the tide of battle when he threw a rock at an American soldier (an event celebrated in Nicaragua today). And at the Second Battle of Rivas, a Costa Rican soldier named Juan Santamaria played a key role in this battle and is today considered to be one of the great military heroes of that country.

Surrounded by four thousand soldiers from Guatemala and El Salvador, Walker ordered his men to burn the city of Granada as they retreated from it. "He incurred the hostility of all Central America through this barbaric and seemingly needless demolition of a cherished metropolis," noted a 1976 book called *Freebooters Must Die: The Life and Death of William Walker.*

Walker and his soldiers (those who hadn't been killed in combat or disease) managed to make it

A playbill for a theatrical production of William Walker's exploits in Nicaragua. *John P. Heiss Papers, Tennessee Historical Society.*

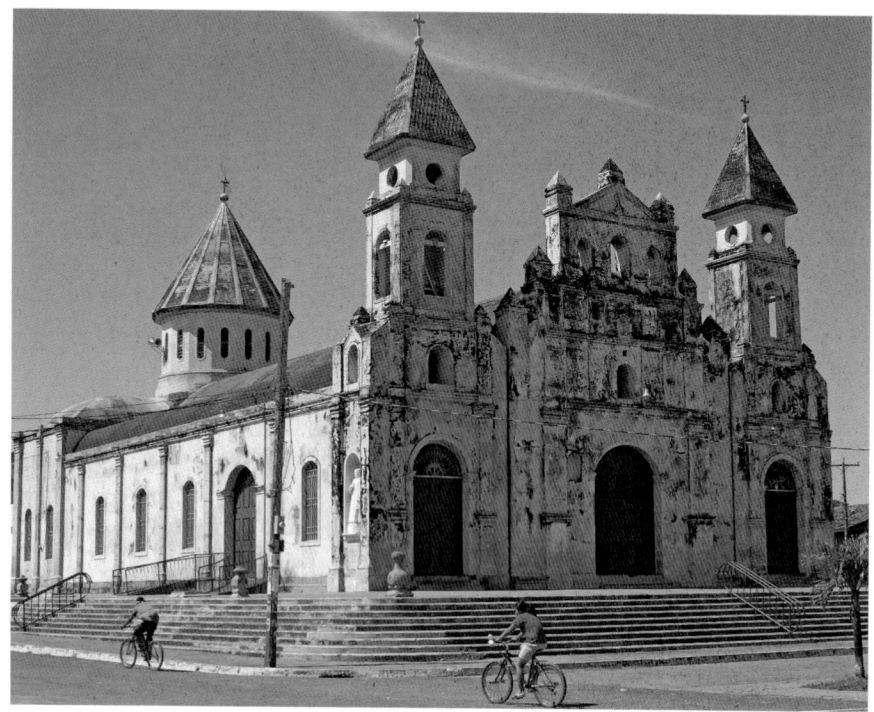

Guadalupe Church in Granada, one of the few structures that survived the burning of the town in 1856. *Kanokratnok/Shutterstock.*

back to the United States. There, Walker was greeted as a hero, especially in the South.

The next year, Walker pulled out of Mobile Bay with 270 men, intending to invade Nicaragua again. However, the expedition was ended by the U.S. Navy, which took Walker and his men into custody and returned them to the United States.

This second "invasion of Nicaragua" reminds us that the U.S. government never supported Walker and his army was never aided by the American military. But the U.S. government was not strong enough on the eve of the Civil War to prevent Walker from raising an army or to keep his ships from leaving U.S. ports in the first place.

In the summer of 1860, Walker tried to invade Honduras. He organized an army of about one hundred men, leaving Mobile Bay with plans to meet up with another ship out of New Orleans. The trip went poorly. Walker's men spent several weeks in Mexico, awaiting the ship from New Orleans that never came. Finally, they landed on Honduran soil near a

Spanish-built fort called Trujillo. After an initial military victory, they surrendered to a British warship, which turned him over to Honduran authorities. On September 12, 1860, William Walker was executed by a Honduran firing squad.

As famous as Walker was in his lifetime, he was largely forgotten after his death, at least in the United States. Only a few months after his execution, the Civil War began in America. Southerners who believed the war would be a short one that would grant them independence to maintain slavery and expand into Central America found out they were gravely wrong.

The people of Central America have, however, not forgotten Walker. He is part of the mandatory school curriculum, and people celebrate many of Walker's defeats as national holidays. Costa Rica celebrates the anniversary of the Second Battle of Rivas every April 11; Nicaragua celebrates the anniversary of the Battle of San Jacinto on September 14.

One more footnote about the Walker saga: About fifteen years after William Walker's death, Cornelius Vanderbilt gave $1 million to the construction of a Methodist university in Nashville. Later called Vanderbilt University, the institution is located a short distance from William Walker's birthplace.

BEAUTY HAULS LOCOMOTIVE

On December 13, 1850, the steamboat *Beauty* hauled something from Cincinnati to Nashville that most Tennesseans had never seen before. It was called a locomotive.

At the time, Nashville was not connected to another city via rail. Everything grown or made in Nashville was either used in Nashville, pulled by horse or floated downriver. But a few years earlier, Tennessee senator James Overton and A.O.P. Nicholson, editor of the *Nashville Union*, had begun organizing support for a new rail line to Chattanooga.

The idea of the railroad was to connect with another railroad, called the Western and Atlantic, then under construction from Savannah to Chattanooga. Known (in theory) as the Nashville and Chattanooga Railroad, it would give Middle Tennessee's farmers access to Atlantic coast markets, plus give Nashville's companies access to untapped coal reserves in southeastern Tennessee.

"The produce of Middle Tennessee, instead of passing over 2,460 miles of dangerous navigation with heavy insurance and many transshipments, would reach Charleston or Savannah in twenty-eight hours…at one-fifth the cost and in one tenth the time," Overton argued.

In 1845, Overton and Nicholson convinced the Tennessee General Assembly to grant their railroad a charter, give it power of eminent domain and to exempt it from taxation for twenty years. They hired Nashville businessman Vernon K. Stevenson to raise money for the project.

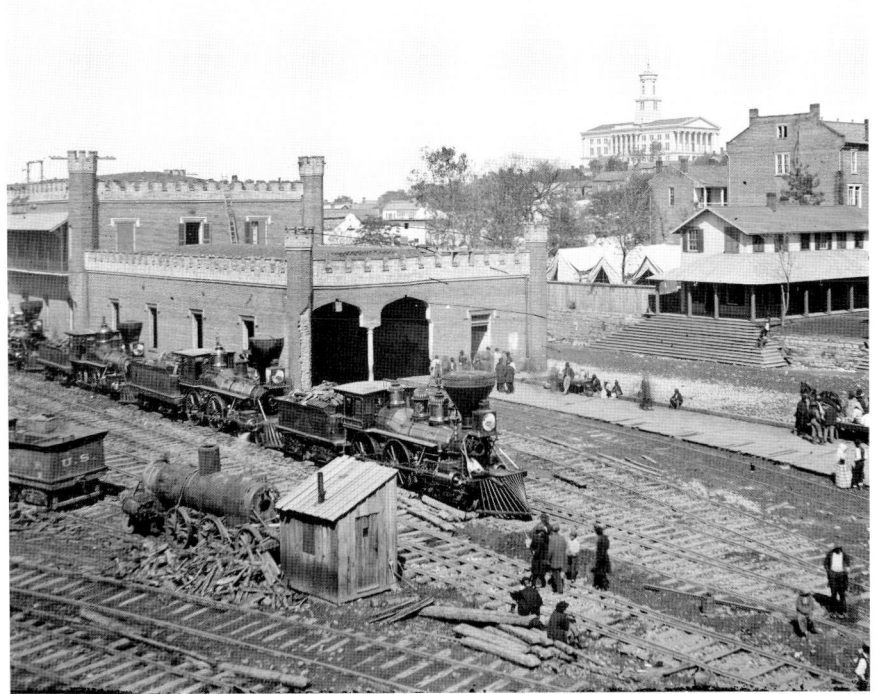

The Nashville and Chattanooga Railroad Depot during the Civil War. *Library of Congress.*

Stevenson went door to door selling stock in the new venture and, in the fall of 1847, raised money in small communities throughout Middle Tennessee such as Fosterville, Wartrace and Winchester. In the end, the governments of Nashville and Charleston, South Carolina, ensured the project's success by investing more than $500,000 each. This investment by Nashville's government was without precedent in Tennessee and was challenged in court, but it was eventually upheld by the Tennessee Supreme Court.

Surveying crews began laying out the rail line in 1847. Since a straight line between Nashville and Chattanooga crossed the Cumberland Plateau at a steep place, engineer John Edgar Thompson chose a 152-mile route through Rutherford, Bedford, Coffee and Franklin Counties and into northeast Alabama, where it turned east at the Tennessee River and headed to Chattanooga from there.

The construction project was monumental and included a 2,200-foot tunnel near a new town in Franklin County called Cowan. "Work was carried on in three shifts," wrote author Wilbur Creighton in *Building of Nashville*. "The drilling was done by hand, since the steam drill had not been perfected at the time. One man would hold and turn a short length of steel bit, while two others struck it with eight-pound hammers."

By the time the *Beauty* brought its enormous cargo upstream in December 1850, Nashville residents were quite excited at the prospect of rail travel. Along with the locomotive, the steamboat brought thirteen freight cars and one passenger car, which impressed a reporter

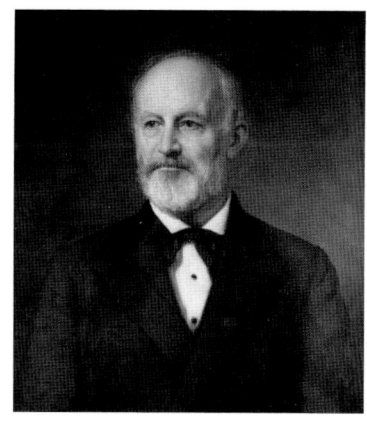

Vernon K. Stevenson. *George Healy,* artist.

from Nashville's afternoon newspaper. "The passenger car is a very beautiful piece of workmanship, the seats of mahogany with figured plush cushions," the *Republican Banner* reported.

Mules (always the unheralded heroes in nineteenth-century Tennessee) dragged the locomotive, freight cars and passenger cars to the Nashville and Chattanooga terminal. In the spring of 1851, the train made its first trip, an eleven-mile jaunt to Antioch. It was a glorious and exciting day for Tennessee's state capital; only the important and well-connected got to ride on that first train. The railroad made it to Murfreesboro on July 4, when there was a celebration dinner attended by four thousand people. "Hundreds of ladies were present, waving their handkerchiefs and making all things appear more happy by their smiles," the *Nashville Union* said on July 7, 1851. The railroad made it all the way to a brand-new town called Tullahoma by the following February.

All the while, other railroads were organized as branch lines on the Nashville and Chattanooga. The McMinnville and Manchester Railroad would eventually connect the main Nashville and Chattanooga trunk line to the coal mining community of Bon Air, on top of the Cumberland Plateau. The Winchester and Alabama Railroad was announced about the same time. It would eventually branch off and head to Fayetteville; Huntsville, Alabama; and Decatur, Alabama.

Meanwhile, there were stories about how property values were going up in Tennessee near the railroad, stories about business being on the rise because of the railroad and stories about how railroads were moving products to Nashville (coal, for instance) that had heretofore moved only by boat. "It is remarkable how railroads seem to create business," the *Banner* reported on March 9, 1852. "All is life and bustle in whatever country they penetrate."

There was also plenty of work to be found—jobs with the railroad, jobs with one of the general contractors hired by the railroad and even simple jobs cutting down cedar trees and sawing them into nine-foot-long cross-ties, of which the railroad needed 2,112 *per mile*.

All was well in Middle Tennessee, and it was all very exciting.

SCATTERED IN EVERY DIRECTION

*L*ike every other railroad built in the South, the Nashville and Chattanooga Railroad was built by people who weren't paid very much (certainly by modern standards), who risked their lives and health more than American workers today and who in some cases were enslaved.

Obviously, many of the people who worked on the railroad were professional engineers who had been trained in colleges. But by the end of 1852, the Nashville and Chattanooga Railroad had hired at least one hundred enslaved people to lay track, repair track and do general maintenance between Murfreesboro and Cowan. Meanwhile, a private contractor called Murdoch and Townsend advertised it needed to lease *an additional* five hundred slaves to work on the line between the Tennessee River bridge in northeast Alabama and Chattanooga. That stretch of railroad involved an especially large amount of blasting and moving of rock—for instance, where the railroad wound around Lookout Mountain.

These enslaved people were sent away from their families and households and leased to the railroad for months or even years. The railroad might pay the slaveholder around $150 per year for their labors. The enslaved people would be clothed and fed at the railroad's expense and would probably sleep in tent-like quarters near where they would work.

Meanwhile, there appear to have been more immigrants working on the railroad than slaves. The Nashville and Chattanooga Railroad hired hundreds of Irish immigrants the moment they got off the ship at Castle Garden, New York, and sent them straight to Tennessee. Far away from their homeland,

Notice to Stockholders.

AN election for fifteen Directors to manage the affairs of the Nashville and Chattanooga Railroad Company for the next year, will take place at Murfreesboro, on the 15th inst, and the report of the state of affairs of the company will be read as usual, on the day before the election. Stockholders will be taken on the road to hear the report read on the 14th, or to the election on the 15th and back home on the 15th or 16th, or over the whole road and back on the same days, as they may prefer, free of charge. They will be required to show their stock certificate to the Conductor as evidence of their right to go free on the cars,

☞ Parties travelling under this privillege must have owned their stock 30 days or more.

By order of the Board.
W. A. GLEAVES, Secretary
Nashville and Chattanooga Railroad Co.
December 6, 1852—2w   U TW A

☞ Murfreesborough, Shelbyville, and Winchester papers copy.

To Slave Holders.

THE Nashville & Chattanooga Railroad Company. wish to hire for the next year one hundred and fifty able bodied Negro men, part to lay track for the 1st 4 months and all to repair track after that time. The work is healthy, pay certain and price remunerative.

Apply at Railroad office Nashville to
    ISAAC LEDBETTER, Murf. Depot.
    R. MOFFATT, Shelbyville.
    E. H JORDAN, Decherd Depot.
    THOS. A. SHILCUT, or ⎱ on the road,
    J. GRAMPS.   ⎰

dec 6—1m.   U W A

Nashville *Republican Banner*, December 5, 1852.

sometimes these immigrants had too much to drink after hours.

In October 1850, the *Nashville Union* reported about a riot between Irish and natives, the natives being Tennesseans. "A bad feeling has existed for some time between the two parties, and on Sunday night, having taken a sufficient quantity of rot gut whiskey to arouse their worst passions, a fuss was raised in which several men were badly used up, but fortunately nobody killed." On the next day, locals destroyed the Irish saloon, using something they had plenty of when blasting a railroad: gunpowder. "Such an explosion has never before been witnessed in these parts," the story claimed.

There were work accidents, or course, but most of the time those didn't make the paper. One exception was an Irishman named Barney Patterson, who made the news in October 1852. Patterson, it seems, "had his foot mashed by being run over by a car a few days since at Tullahoma," the *Banner* reported. "He was brought to the state hospital Friday and Saturday amputation was performed on his foot by Dr. Buchanan."

The greater danger was disease. In 1849 and 1850, there were cholera outbreaks all over the United States. The death counts were especially bad in Mississippi River cities such as New Orleans and St. Louis, but it was also awful in Nashville, where an estimated 311 people died from the disease. (The most famous of the casualties was James K. Polk.)

On or about July 16, 1850, cholera spread through among railroad workers working on the Nashville and Chattanooga Railroad tunnel, south of Cowan. According to a story in the *Winchester Independent*, the first victim was a woman named Mrs. Mills, who died about a day after she fell ill. The second death was Edward Paul, a native of Cornwall, England, and one of the superintendents on the tunnel construction. "He was a married man, and he expected his wife here from Pennsylvania in today's stage," the newspaper reported. By the time this small item went to press, six other people died of cholera, including one child.

Today, we don't know whether printed accounts of this outbreak are exaggerated. But what the *Winchester Independent* reported on July 26 is horrible to contemplate. "At the beginning of the cholera, the hands and families living at the tunnel were dispersed and scattered in every direction, there was no security in flight; the fell [cruel] disease followed them up and cut them down wherever they went."

On August 2, the *Independent* listed the names of twenty-eight people near the tunnel who died of disease, including four enslaved people and six children. However, the newspaper maintained that the town of Winchester (only seven miles away) had escaped the scourge. It made no mention of law enforcement efforts the town had made to keep diseased workers away from the town, although no doubt there would have been some.

Only a few weeks later, the *Banner* sent a reporter to Cowan. The reporter said "a number" of cabins had been burned in the communities where workers lived, as it was common practice to burn down the cabins of people who died of cholera—often with their bodies still in them. The reporter also said thirty-one workers had died of cholera "out of a population of one hundred and eighty."

All of this reminded me that there is an abandoned Irish cemetery along the railroad tracks, above Cowan. I've never seen it (it's difficult to reach and on private property), but oral history maintains there are many unmarked graves of cholera victims there.

Then there were the accidents. As one leg after another of the railroad opened, train crashes occurred with surprising regularity. The first accident took place in October 1851, when a locomotive, passenger car and freight car ran off the tracks at Overall Creek in Rutherford County. "It is astonishing that every person on them was not killed, as the locomotive turned over once or twice," the *Banner* reported. "There were but a few passengers in the cars fortunately, and they crawled out through the bottom." The only person killed was an African American man, almost certainly an enslaved one, whose name didn't even make the paper.

The following January, a train ran off the bridge at Brown's Creek, in Davidson County. The train fell an estimated sixty feet, but, incredibly, no one was hurt.

In August 1852 came the third big accident. A locomotive heading northwest in Davidson County hit a cow, which obviously didn't survive. As for the train, "the locomotive and cars rubbed over, dragging her [the cow] some distance," the paper reported. "The rear car was thrown off the track and turned over."

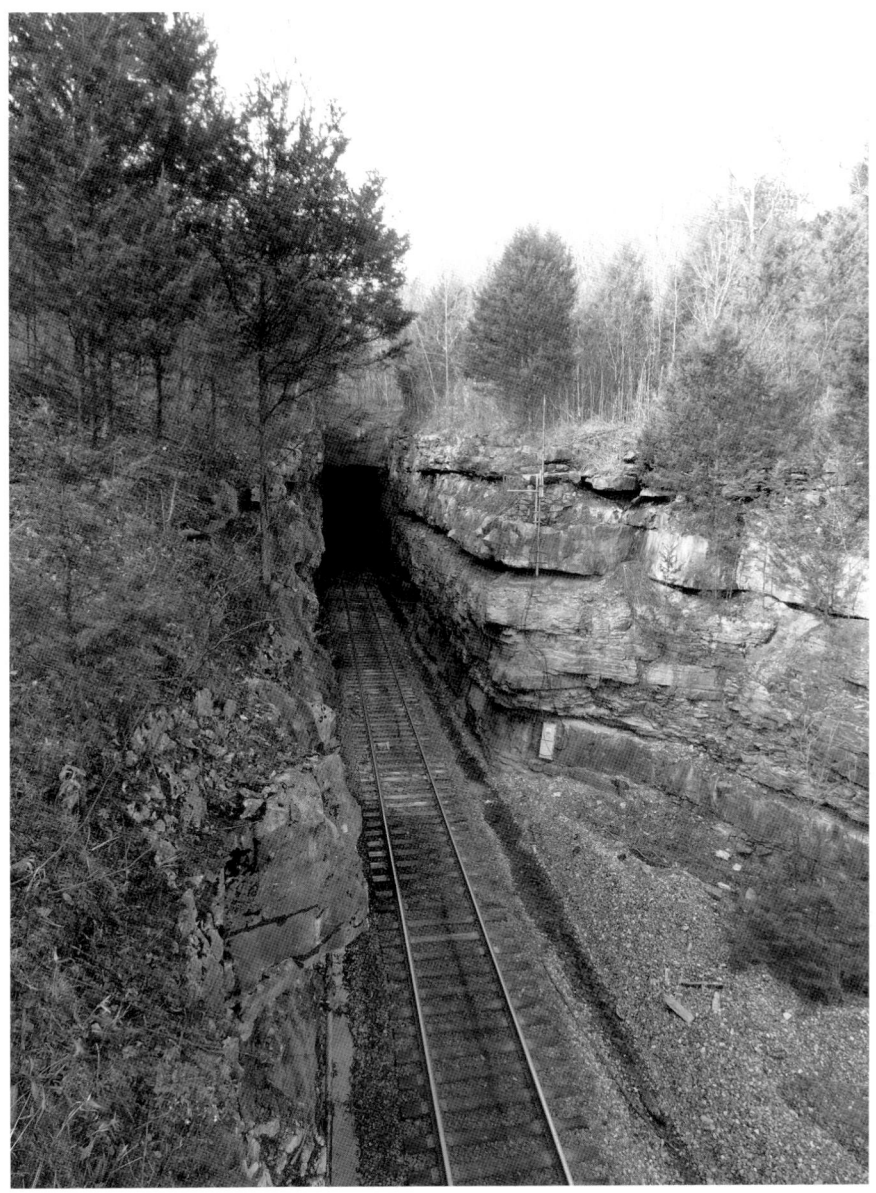

The Nashville and Chattanooga Railroad tunnel near Cowan. *Bryan MacKinnon.*

Five months later, an actual collision occurred on the railroad, which led the *Winchester Independent* to opine that maybe some safety procedures might be in order. "Accidents on this [rail] road are becoming so common that little notice is taken of them. It does seem to us that some measure could be adopted to prevent *collisions* at least."

HONEST AND UNSUSPECTING STOCKHOLDERS

*T*hroughout Nashville history, most business have kept their internal squabbles to themselves. There were arguments involving the people who ran Cumberland Telephone and Telegraph, Genesco, Hospital Corporation of America and all the other important companies in Nashville history. But for the most part, these disagreements and accusations took place behind closed doors or in private correspondences.

In 1852, the Nashville and Chattanooga Railroad was behind schedule and over budget for several reasons. Getting workers was a problem. Yes, there were a lot of Irish immigrants who could be (and were) recruited to work on the railroad; companies contracted by the Nashville and Chattanooga Railroad hired immigrants by the hundreds at the debarkation point at Castle Island, New York. But there were a lot of other railroads being built in the United States then, so there was competition over them.

Engineering was a problem. Parts of the Cumberland Plateau were hard to cut through, and the Tennessee River was hard to cross. Disease was also a problem. During the course of construction, workers had suffered outbreaks of cholera, smallpox and typhoid fever. The railroad was so over budget, in fact, that the State of Tennessee bailed it out—the General Assembly agreeing in 1852 to purchase $650,000 in bonds backed by the railroad.

Then, on October 17, 1853, the railroad's dirty laundry was aired. On that day, the *Republican Banner* ran an angry letter by Bedford County resident James L. Armstrong, addressed to his fellow stockholders of the Nashville

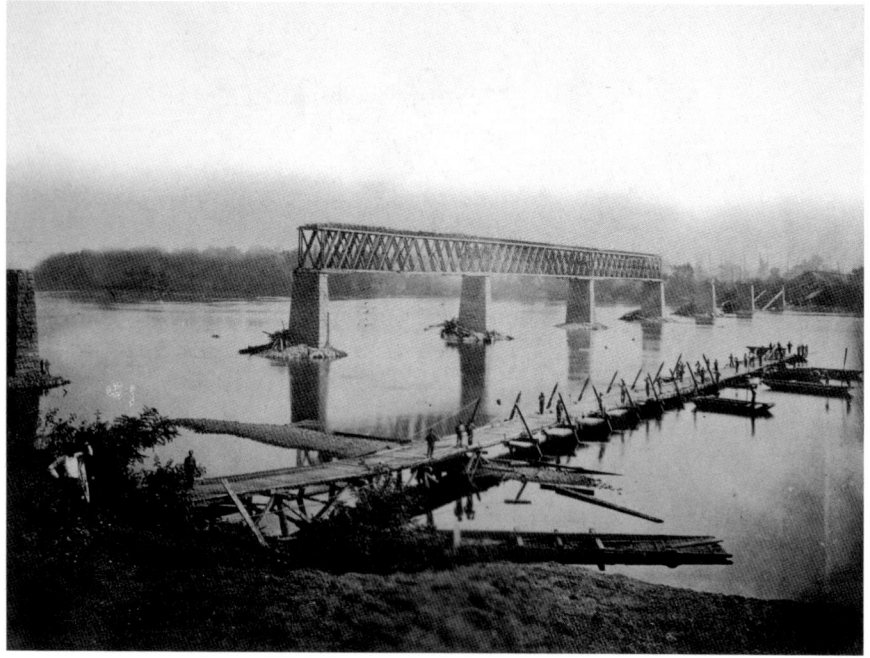

The Nashville and Chattanooga Railroad bridge at Bridgeport was photographed after it was destroyed in the Civil War. *Library of Congress.*

and Chattanooga Railroad. The letter accused two N&C executives—President Vernon Stevenson and Treasurer Peter Decherd in particular—of impropriety in the running of the railroad. It's a long letter—about five thousand words in length. Among Armstrong's accusations:

- The reason the railroad's Nashville depot was moved from one part of town to another was because Stevenson owned a lot of real estate near the second location.
- A depot on the railroad known as Christiana was put there to please a "pet engineer, named [George] Hazlehurst, who owned the land."
- The depot in Shelbyville was put where one of the railroad's directors owned land.
- The depot at Tullahoma was located where it was because Stevenson's brother owned land there.
- A depot was intentionally placed on land owned by Peter Decherd so he could make more money from a town he developed on the site.

- Stevenson chose to put the railroad's most important depot—
  the one where the railroad hits its most southern latitude at
  the Tennessee River in Alabama before turning east toward
  Chattanooga—in a "swamp, a real Crow Creek swamp…
  because it was the land of the president—when by going a
  short distance further, there is one of the best sites for a depot
  that I have ever seen on the road."

Armstrong concluded his letter by pointing out that the estimate cost
of the railroad had risen from $2.46 million in December 1849 to $2.94
million in December 1852 to $3.60 million in May 1853. "And yet this
[Stevenson] is the great financier, who is the only person in all Tennessee,
capable of carrying on such a work, and protecting the immense capital

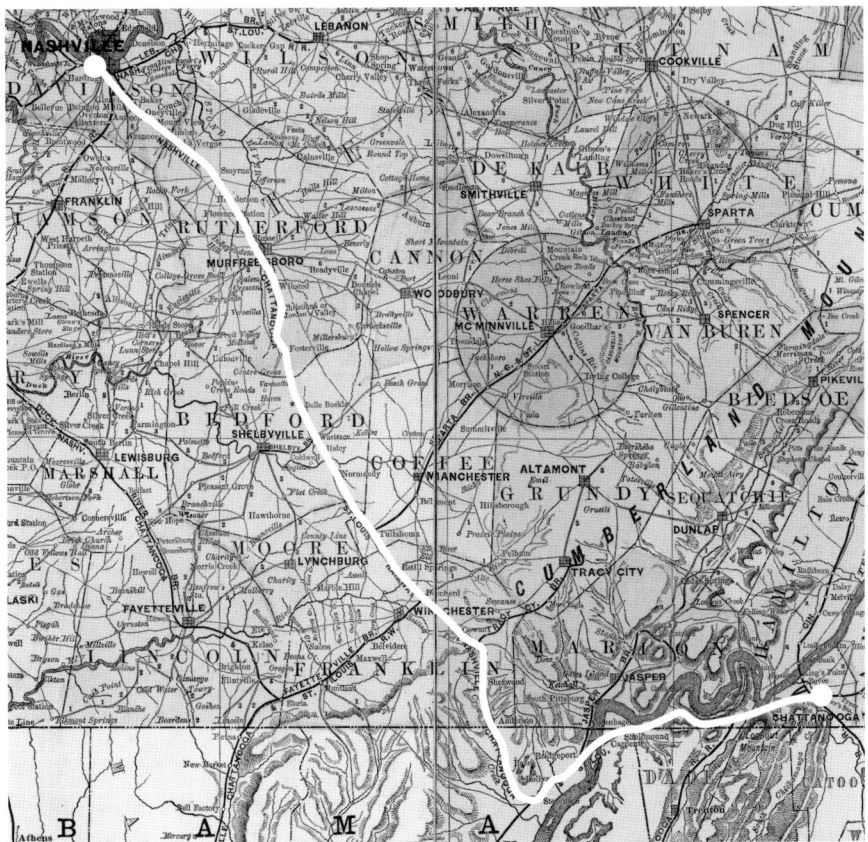

The route taken by the Nashville and Chattanooga Railroad. *Rand, McNally & Company
map, 1888.*

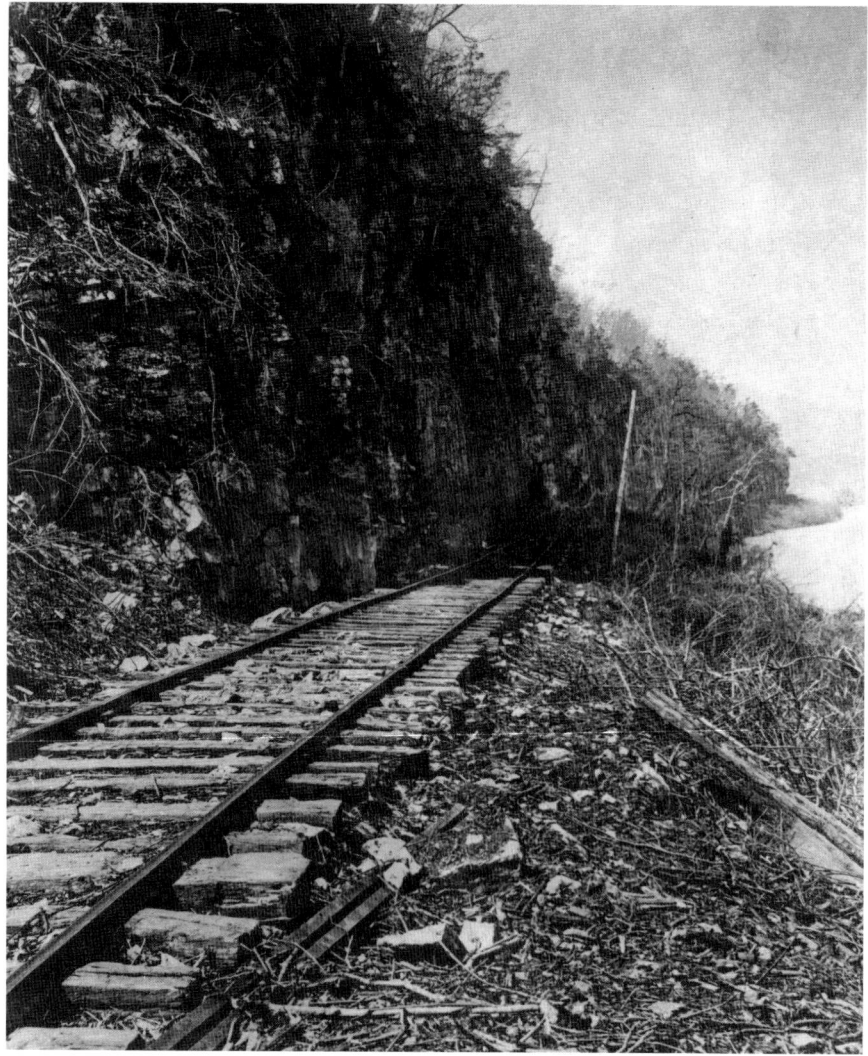

The Nashville and Chattanooga Railroad tracks at the foot of Lookout Mountain. *Library of Congress.*

of the honest and unsuspecting stockholders, invested in this great enterprise."

Stevenson's lengthy response to Armstrong's letter was published in the *Banner* two days later. He started off by saying Armstrong's letter had been "written in a spirit of malevolence and disappointed aspiration" but he was "grateful" for his chance to answer the charges. One at a time, Stevenson addressed the specific accusations about real estate decisions.

In regards to downtown Nashville, "no change was every made with the location of that depot, and the only piece of property owned by me on that street is a residence…which has been injured in value as a residence rather than benefitted by the depot."

The accusations regarding the Christiana depot and Mr. Hazlehurst were also unfounded, Stevenson wrote. "Murfreesboro having been made a station, it became necessary to have another at a distance of about 10 miles beyond that point.…This precise distance having been found to have an ascending grade where it is difficult and expensive to keep up a station, and Fosterville, which is the head of grade, being three miles off, which was too far to meet the necessities of the locomotives, an intermediate and level situation between 10 miles from Murfreesboro and Fosterville, where would and water could be procured, was the only alternative."

Stevenson went on and on, addressing the Shelbyville depot, the Tullahoma depot, the Decherd depot and the Stevenson depot. As for cost overruns, he acknowledged they had occurred, but he pointed out, "There has been less of failure and disappointment in the construction of the Chattanooga Railroad than in any other enterprise of the same magnitude undertaken in this country.…It was begun in 1848, and it is now within two months of its final completion, occupying its erection a period of only 5 years. It crosses a more mountainous region than any, except three roads, in the United States. It spans a river as large nearly, if not larger, than any one hitherto passed by a locomotive in the Union, and it was a new species of enterprise in Tennessee."

He then cited the Erie Railroad—"estimate at a cost of $7 million and has really expended $40 million"—the Pennsylvania Railroad and the Baltimore and Ohio Railroad as examples of enterprises that went much further over budget than the Nashville and Chattanooga.

Stevenson concluded by writing, "I have thus given a brief answer to all the charges made by Dr. Armstrong, and leave it to the public to form their own judgment. It is not claimed by the president of the [rail] road that he is unerring, or that the directory are infallible; all they assert is, that they have endeavored faithfully to meet their responsibility, and have always acted in the best manner their united judgments could dictate."

The charges went back and forth in the Nashville press for some time afterward. It certainly gave everyone something to talk about, and I suspect it sold a lot of newspapers.

So, on the one hand, the Nashville and Chattanooga Railroad had its share of wonderful achievements—the first ride from Nashville to Antioch and the opening of the tunnel in Cowan, for instance. But it also encountered tragedies, such as the cholera pandemic and the early train accidents. And it needs to be remembered that many of the men blasting rock, moving dirt, hauling logs into place and hammering in rails were enslaved, while many others were immigrants in a new land.

The accidents, the delays, the epidemics, the labor problem, the cost overruns and the public arguments between Stevenson and Armstrong may account for the following: When Nashville was finally connected to Chattanooga, the newspapers treated it with more relief than celebration. On Saturday, January 15, 1854, the locomotive *Tennessee* crossed the Nashville and Chattanooga Railroad bridge over the Tennessee River, just east of the town that later became known as Bridgeport, Alabama. The train rolled into Chattanooga two days later. "Henceforth there will be uninterrupted communication by railroad between Nashville and Montgomery, AL, Charleston and Savannah," the *Banner* reported—not bothering to mention Atlanta because it wasn't very big yet.

Forty-three years had passed since the ground literally shook during the New Madrid earthquakes. With the arrival of the locomotive in Chattanooga, the Tennessee earth shook again, for about the fifth time in half a century. It was no longer the same state it had been. Not much of a state in 1800, with only about 100,000 people, Tennessee had 1 million people fifty years later and had produced two American presidents who had served a combined twelve years. The Chickasaws and Cherokees were gone, forced out. The steamboat had come, made the keelboat look like it was standing still and changed commerce and pace of life. The telegraph brought the news of the world in a matter of seconds. And now the railroad had arrived, and Nashville was only a comfortable train ride to the Atlantic Ocean.

I'm sure it was hard for people who were alive in 1854 to get their minds around all the changes they had seen in their lifetimes. They had no conception of what misery was brewing for the next decade.

SOURCES

Books/Essays

Arthur, Stanley Clisby. *The Story of the Battle of New Orleans*. New Orleans: Louisiana Historical Society, 1915.

Baker, John F., Jr. *The Washingtons of Wessyngton Plantation: Stories of My Family's Journey to Freedom*. New York: Atria Books, 2009.

Bancroft, Frederick. *Slave Trading in the Old South*. New York: Frederick Ungar Publishing Company, 1931.

Borneman, Walter. Polk: *The Man Who Transformed the Presidency and America*. New York: Random House, 2008.

Brands, H.W. *Andrew Jackson: His Life and Times*. New York: Doubleday, 2005.

Brown, John P. *Old Frontiers: The Story of the Cherokee Indians from the Earliest Times to the Date of Their Removal to the West*. Kingsport, TN: Souther Publishers, 1938.

Carey, Bill. *Runaways, Coffles and Fancy Girls: A History of Slavery in Tennessee*. Nashville, TN: Clearbrook Press, 2018.

Clayton, W.W. *History of Davidson County, Tennessee, with Illustrations and Biographical Sketches of Its Prominent Men and Pioneers*. Philadelphia, PA: J.W. Lewis & Company, 1880.

Creighton, Wilbur. *Building of Nashville*. Nashville, TN: Wilbur F. Creighton, 1969.

Crockett, David. *A Narrative of the Life of David Crockett of the State of Tennessee*. Knoxville: University of Tennessee Press, 1973.

Day, Donald, and Harry Herbert Ullum. *The Autobiography of Sam Houston.* Norman: University of Oklahoma Press, 1947.

Dilts, James D. *The Great Road: The Building of the Baltimore and Ohio, the Nation's First Railroad, 1828–1853.* Stanford, CA: Stanford University Press, 1993.

Ehle, John. *Trail of Tears: The Rise and Fall of the Cherokee Nation.* New York: Random House, 1988.

Featherstonhaugh, G.W. *Excursion through the Slave States.* London: John Murray, 1844.

Fuller, Myron. *The New Madrid Earthquake.* Washington, D.C.: U.S. Geological Survey, 1912.

Goodstein, Anita Shafer. *Nashville, 1780–1860: From Frontier to City.* Gainesville: University of Florida Press, 1989.

Greenberg, Amy S. *Lady First: The World of First Lady Sarah Polk.* New York: Alfred A. Knopf, 2019.

Hoig, Stan. *Sequoyah: The Cherokee Genius.* Oklahoma City: Oklahoma Historical Society, 1995.

Knox, Jack. *Riverman, with Pen and Ink Sketches by the Author.* Nashville, TN: Abingdon Press, 1971.

Latrobe, John H.B. "A Lost Chapter in the History of the Steamboat." A paper presented to the Maryland Historical Society in 1871.

McKenzie, Robert Tracy. *Lincolnites and Rebels: A Divided Town in the Civil War.* Oxford, MS: Oxford University Press, 2006.

Monaghan, Jay. *The Great Rascal: The Life and Adventures of Ned Buntline.* New York: Bonanza Books, 1951.

Myer, William E. *Indian Trails of the Southeast.* Nashville, TN: Blue & Gray Press, 1971.

Olmsted, Frederick Law. *A Journey in the Seaboard Slave States.* Charleston, SC: Arcadia Publishing, 2017.

Penick, James Lal, Jr. *The Great Western Land Pirate: John A. Murrell in Legend and History.* Columbia: University of Missouri Press, 1981.

———. *The New Madrid Earthquakes.* Columbia: University of Missouri Press, 1971.

Pfister, Harold Francis. *Facing the Light: Historic American Portrait Daguerreotypes.* Washington, D.C.: Smithsonian Institute Press, 1978.

Rosengarter, Frederic, Jr. *Freebooters Must Die: The Life and Death of William Walker.* Wayne, PA: Haverford House, 1976.

Schult, Dain L. *Nashville, Chattanooga and St. Louis: A History of the Dixie Line.* Lynchburg, VA: TLC Publishing, 2002.

Seward, William H. *William H. Seward: An Autobiography*. New York: Derby and Miller, 1891.

Silverman, Kenneth. *Lightning Man: The Accursed Life of Samuel F.B. Morse*. New York: Alfred Knopf, 2003.

Stowe, Harriet Beecher. *The Key to* Uncle Tom's Cabin*: Presenting the Original Facts and Documents Upon Which the Story Is Founded*. Boston: John P. Jewett and Company, 1854.

Watson, Henry. *A Narrative of the Life of Henry Watson, a Fugitive Slave*. Boston: Bela Marsh, 1848.

Wellman, Paul I. *Spawn of Evil*. New York: Pyramid Books, 1964.

Woodall, Eliza B. *The Stevenson Story*. Stevenson, AL: Stevenson Depot Museum, 1982.

Newspaper Articles (by Chapter)

GROUND RISES AND FALLS
Charleston Daily Courier, December 17, 1811.

UP PAST THE SHOALS
Clarion and Tennessee Gazette, June 23; September 1, November 10 and December 1, 1818; January 5, 1819.
Knoxville Enquirer, February 13, 1819.
Nashville Whig, April 30, 1816; March 7, 1818; March 13, 1819; June 6, 1821.
National Banner and Nashville Whig, January 26, February 16 and March 15, 1818.
Pittsburgh Weekly Gazette, March 10, 1818.

WEALTHY, RESPECTABLE AND POPULOUS
Jackson Gazette, August 24, 1824; January 10, February 12 and 19, June 11 and July 9, 1825; November 6 and December 23, 1826.
Nashville Republican, December 29, 1836.
Nashville Whig, September 25, 1818; August 28, 1822; February 21, 1825.
Pittsburgh Weekly Gazette, July 3, 1820.

A TRACE OF TRUTH
Knoxville Gazette, April 6, and June 22, 1808.
Nashville Banner, July 3, 1934.
Nashville Clarion, April 26, 1808; June 16, 1818; April 25, 1821.

Nashville Whig, March 1, 1820.

Tennessean, September 2, 1974.

Tennessee Gazette and Mero Advertiser, February 11, 1801; August 24, 1803; May 30, 1804; March 28, 1807.

Born in the Waxhaws

Philadelphia Inquirer, November 19, 1794.

Without Any Just Cause

Fayetteville Observer, September 17, 1857.

Jackson Gazette, June 12, 1824.

Knoxville Gazette, April 7, 1792.

Mero District Advertiser, November 9, 1805.

Nashville Whig, May 31, 1814; December 12, 1825.

Republican Banner, January 14, 1836.

Letters Etched in Stone

Arkansas Gazette, May 30, 1832.

Arkansas Times, April 25, 1834.

Clarksville Tobacco Leaf, October 3 and November 11, 1878.

Fayetteville Weekly Observer, November 19, 1833.

Nashville Banner, June 17, 1833.

Nashville Daily American, March 22, 1876.

Nashville Whig, April 16 and November 12, 1816; March 26, April 23 and May 19, 1817; May 16, June 2 and December 19, 1818; February 6 and June 5, 1819; February 14, June 23, July 7, October 24 and November 6, 1821; February 6, 1822; September 22, 1823; November 19 and December 13, 1824; October 3, 1825.

National Banner/Whig, January 1, April 9 and June 7, 1830; November 11 and December 22, 1831; February 3 and November 26, 1832; January 23, 1834.

Republican Banner, September 6, 1836; August 27, 1847.

Stewart County Times, February 16, 1954.

Four Days from Nashville to Knoxville

Knoxville Argus, January 19, 1844.

Knoxville Gazette, January 9, 1795.

Knoxville Register, May 29, 1829; March 24, 1830; June 20, 1832.

(Nashville) *Republican Banner*, April 8, 1851; July 21, 1853.

Nashville Whig, May 5, 1817; December 1, 1823; April 19, 1824.

National Banner and Nashville Whig, January 15, 1830; June 8, 1833; June 26, 1838.
State Gazette of N.C., December 18, 1788.

MANACLED AND CHAINED
Knoxville Register, May 8, 1833.
Nashville Whig, May 1, 1819; April 17, 1822; August 6, 1825.
Natchez Gazette, April 26, 1826.
New Orleans Weekly Delta, December 28, 1846.
Republican Banner, May 6, 1846.

MEMPHIS RIVAL VANISHES FROM THE MAP
Randolph Recorder, 1834–36 (all surviving issues on microfilm at the Tennessee
    State Library and Archives).

DISNEY MOVIES AND COONSKIN CAPS/CROCKETT LOSES HIS PANTS
Jackson Gazette, September 23, 1826; May 5, 1827.

LAND PIRATE'S THUMB
Herald Mail, February 4, 1876.

RED CLAY'S SOMBER STORY/BAREFOOT AND BADLY CLAD
Athens Journal, December 22, 1836; June 8, 1838.
Baltimore American, January 25, 1838.
Chattanooga Daily Times, August 25, 1963.
Democratic Free Press, July 18, 1838.
Fayetteville Weekly, November 28, 1838.
Georgia Pioneer, October 30, 1838.
Hamilton Gazette, October 1, 1838.
Knoxville Register, July 18, 1838.
(Lexington) *Kentucky Gazette*, October 11, 1838.
(Macon, Georgia) *Weekly Telegraph*, September 18, 1838.
Nashville Republican, May 5, 1837; December 1, 1838.
Nashville Union, April 21, May 23 and August 15, 1838.
Nashville Whig, October 24, 1838.
Natchez Weekly Courier, November 23, 1838.
Newbern (NC) Spectator, September 28, 1838.
Republican Banner, August 29, October 9 and 16, November 5 and December
    11, 1838.
Tennessee Baptist, December 1, 1838.

ENGINEER PUTS CHATTANOOGA ON THE MAP
Republican Banner, September 18, 1839.

THIS POLITICAL SODOM
Brownlow's Knoxville Whig, January 9, 1864.
Clarksville Weekly, October 10, 1843.
Knoxville Register, November 18, 1843.
Nashville Union, October 7 and 9, 1843.
Republican Banner, October 4, 6 and 9 and November 17, 1843; May 16, 1850.

LIARS, COWARDS AND POLTROONS
Brownlow's Knoxville Whig, March 6, 1852; October 17, 1860.
Jonesborough Whig, October 21, 1840; April 7, 1841; September 22, 1841; December 13, 1843.
Knoxville Whig, October 17, 1860.
Nashville Impartial Review and Cumberland Repository, April 25, 1807.
Raleigh Weekly Standard, August 10, 1853.
Tennessee Gazette, October 26, 1803.
Tennessee Whig, January 30 and May 14, 1840.

NED BUNTLINE'S ROPE
Abbeville Press, August 4, 1886.
Lincoln County Journal, June 19, 1846.
Pulaski Citizen, July 29, 1886.
Tri Weekly Nashville Union, March 17–18, 1846.

BRITANNIA ARRIVES AT BOSTON
Baltimore Sun, May 7, 25, 27 and 28, 1844.
Nashville Daily Union, January 4, 5 and 25, February 23 and 26 and March 4, 7, 8 and 15, 1848.

PRESIDENT LEAVES A MESS OF A LEGACY
Knoxville Register, September 28, 1819; September 25, 1821; August 27, 1824.
Nashville American, September 9, 1875; August 17 and October 10, 1891; May 25, June 28, July 13, August 27 and December 20, 1892; September 20, 1893; June 15, 19 and 27, 1897; October 7 and November 14, 1899; April 10, November 3 and December 5, 1900.
Nashville Banner, March 12, 1898.

Nashville Gazette, April 4, 1823.

Nashville Union, February 15, 1870.

Nashville Whig, March 12, 1823; January 12, 1824.

Raleigh Weekly Register, July 11, 1817.

Republican Banner, June 18, 1849; February 20, 1873; May 6, 1874; October 31, 1874.

Wichita Times, December 15, 1894.

Wichita Weekly Eagle, March 30, 1876.

TENNESSEE'S CONNECTION TO *UNCLE TOM'S CABIN*

Anti-Slavery Bugle, August 10, 1850.

Caledonia Mercury, July 26, 1849.

Liberator, May 18, 1849.

(London, England) *Lloyd's Weekly*, July 15, 1849.

Mansfield (OH) News Journal, June 14, 1964.

Nashville Daily Union, December 7, 1848; April 13 and 30, 1849.

Republican Banner, July 2, 1850.

BEAUTY HAULS LOCOMOTIVE/SCATTERED AT EVERY DIRECTION/HONEST AND UNSUSPECTING SHAREHOLDERS

Athens Post, September 13, 1850; December 20, 1850; March 7, 1851; May 21, 1852; February 17, 1854.

Buffalo Commercial, June 9, 1848.

Charleston Courier, August 9, 1850; November 17, 1853.

Charleston Mercury, February 13, 1854.

Eufala Spirit, December 11, 1849.

Huntsville (AL) Democrat, August 15, 1850.

Loudoun Free Press, November 13, 1852; November 18, 1853; January 23, 1854.

Nashville Union/Nashville Daily Union, July 17, 1845; June 20 and 29, 1846; March 25 and December 8 and 10, 1847; December 18 and 23, 1848; December 22, 1849; March 22, July 23 and 30, August 13, September 2 and 3 and October 8 and 31, 1850; February 10, August 23 and 25 and December 3, 1851; January 27, March 24, November 9 and 16 and December 16 and 22, 1852; January 1, March 20, May 17 and 21, June 30, September 9 and November 23, 1853; January 11 and 17 and February 20, 1854.

New York Daily Herald, June 11, 1847.

Pulaski Gazette, November 5, 1852.

Republican Banner/Daily Republican Banner, June 26, 1846; March 1, 1847; September 3, 1847; October 10, 1847; August 4, November 17 and December 8, 1848; January 17, May 29, August 19, October 2 and December 14 and 16, 1850; January 31, February 12, April 26, June 18, August 12, 15 and 29, September 5, October 29, November 7 and December 6, 1851; February 12 and 27, March 9, May 4, August 14 and 28, October 4, Novemebr 22 and December 1, 18 and 21, 1852; January 8 and 17, February 15, 17 and 23, March 17, May 3–6, May 26, June 6 and 23, July 20 and October 17 and 19, 1853; January 16, 20 and 28, 1854; August 1, 1868.

INDEX

H

I

J

K

King, Duane 29
Kingsport, TN 59
Kingston, TN 53, 59, 65, 104, 105, 106
Know Nothing Party 117, 120
Knox County, TN 46
Knoxville, TN 19, 20, 43, 52, 59, 60, 61, 65, 104, 105, 106, 109

L

LaGrange, TN 62
Lake Nicaragua 138
Lane, Harriet 113, 114
La Paz, Mexico 137
La Roche, Firmin 14
Laughlin, Samuel 107
Lawrenceburg, TN 129
Lawrence County Courthouse 75
Lawrence County, TN 40, 52, 74, 75
Lebanon, TN 106
Leiper's Fork, TN 41
Lewis County, TN 39
Lewis, Meriwether 39, 52
Lexington, TN 35
Lincoln, Abraham 45, 66, 133
Lincoln County, TN 47, 74
Lion of the West (play) 75
Little Tennessee River 98
Livingston, Robert 16
Long, Stephen Harriman 100–103
Lookout Mountain 146
Loosahatchie River 36
Louisiana 28, 63, 67
Louisiana Purchase 137
Louisville, KY 11, 20, 62, 102, 103, 125
Lowery, George 32

Lundy, Samuel 111
Lynchburg, TN 62

M

Madison County, TN 81
Madison, Dolley 113, 115
Madison, James 113
Magnetic Telegraph Company 125
Manchester, TN 106
Marshall, John 92
Marshal, Park 40
Marthasville, GA 102
Maryland 29, 64
Maryville, TN 60
Mason, John Y. 115
Maury County Courthouse 129
Maury County, TN 40, 52, 107, 128
McClanahan, J. Craig 131
McMinnville and Manchester Railroad 144
McMinnville, TN 60, 106
McNairy County, TN 36, 40, 53
Memphis, TN 16, 18, 34, 35, 50, 61, 62, 69, 71, 72, 77, 80
Menawa 22
Mexico 33, 130, 140
Mill Creek (Davidson County, TN) 58, 98, 99
Mississippi 63
Mississippi River 12, 13, 16, 18, 21, 25–28, 34, 37, 63, 69–72, 75, 78, 79, 80, 81, 86, 89, 90, 92, 93, 95, 99, 147
Mississippi River Corridor 72
Missouri 11
Mobile, AL 22
Mobile Bay 140

ABOUT THE AUTHOR

*B*ill Carey was a reporter in the 1990s and at various times worked for the *Tennessean, Nashville Scene* and nashvillepost.com, which he cofounded. He has authored, among other books, *Fortunes, Fiddles, and Fried Chicken: A Nashville Business History* and *Runaways, Coffles and Fancy Girls: A History of Slavery in Tennessee.* In 2004, Carey started Tennessee History for Kids, a nonprofit organization that helps public school teachers with Tennessee history and social studies. Somehow, he also finds time to write a monthly history column for *Tennessee Magazine* and a weekly history column published in about forty-five Tennessee newspapers. Bill has two grown children and lives in Williamson County with his wife, teenage son and a cattle dog, Riley, with whom he runs daily.